DISCOURSE ON COLONIALISM

DISCOURSE ON COLONIALISM

Aimé Césaire

Translated by Joan Pinkham

A POETICS OF ANTICOLONIALISM

by Robin D.G. Kelley

MR

MONTHLY REVIEW PRESS
NEW YORK

Originally published as *Discours sur le colonialisme* by Présence Africaine,
Copyright ©1955 by Editions Présence Africaine

Library of Congress Cataloging-in-Publication Data

Césaire Aimé.
    [Discours sur le colonialisme. English]
    Discourse on colonialism / Aimé Césaire; translated by Joan Pinkham.
    A poetics of anticolonialism / Robin D.G. Kelley.
        p. cm.
    Contents: A poetics of anticolonialism / Robin D.G. Kelley —
    Discourse on colonialism / Aimé Césaire — An interview with Aimé Césaire /
    René Depestre.
    ISBN 1-58367-025-4 (pbk.) — ISBN 1-58367-024-6 (cloth)
    1. Colonies. 2. Colonies—Africa. 3. Postcolonialism. I. Kelley, Robin D.G.
Poetics of anticolonialism. II. Title: Poetics of anticolonialism. III. Title.

JV51 .C413 2000
325'.3—dc21   00-020238
                                                    CIP

Monthly Review Press
122 West 27th Street
New York, NY 10001

Printed in Canada

10 9 8 7 6 5 4 3 2 1

[Contents]

A POETICS OF ANTICOLONIALISM

Robin D.G. Kelley

Aimé Césaire's *Discourse on Colonialism* might be best described as a declaration of war. I would almost call it a "third world manifesto," but hesitate because it is primarily a polemic against the old order bereft of the kind of propositions and proposals that generally accompany manifestos. Yet, *Discourse* speaks in revolutionary cadences, capturing the spirit of its age just as Marx and Engels did 102 years earlier in their little manifesto. First published in 1950 as *Discours sur le colonialisme*, it appeared just as the old empires were on the verge of collapse, thanks in part to a world war against fascism that left Europe in material, spiritual, and philosophical shambles.[1] It was the age of decolonization and revolt in Africa, Asia, and Latin America. Five years earlier, in 1945, black people from around the globe gathered in Manchester, England, for the Fifth Pan-African Congress to discuss the freedom and future of Africa. Five years later, in 1955, representatives from the Non-Aligned Nations gathered in

Bandung, Indonesia, to discuss the freedom and future of the third world. Mao's revolution in China was a year old, while the Mau Mau in Kenya were just gearing up for an uprising against their colonial masters. The French encountered insurrections in Algeria, Tunisia, Morocco, Cameroon, and Madagascar, and suffered a humiliating defeat by the Viet Minh at Dien Bien Phu. Revolt was in the air. India, the Philippines, Guyana, Egypt, Guatemala, South Africa, Alabama, Mississippi, Georgia, Harlem, you name it. Revolt! Malcolm X once described this extraordinary moment, this long decade from the end of the Second World War to the late 1950s, as a "tidal wave of color."

Discourse on Colonialism is indisputably one of the key texts in this "tidal wave" of anticolonial literature produced during the postwar period—works that include W.E.B. Du Bois's *Color and Democracy* (1945) and *The World and Africa* (1947), Frantz Fanon's *Black Skin, White Masks* (1952), George Padmore's *Pan-Africanism or Communism?: The Coming Struggle for Africa* (1956), Albert Memmi's *The Colonizer and the Colonized* (1957), Richard Wright's *White Man Listen!* (1957), Jean-Paul Sartre's essay, "Black Orpheus" (1948), and journals such as *Présence Africaine* and *African Revolution*. Like much of the radical literature produced during this epoch, *Discourse* places the colonial question front and center. Although Césaire, remaining somewhat true to his Communist affiliation, never quite dethrones the modern proletariat from its exalted status as a revolutionary force, the European working class is practically invisible. This is a book about colonialism, its impact on the colonized, on culture, on history, on the very concept of civilization itself, and most importantly, on the colonizer. In the finest Hegelian fashion, Césaire demonstrates how colonialism works to "decivilize" the colonizer: torture, violence, race hatred, and immorality constitute a dead weight on the so-called civilized, pulling the master class deeper and deeper into the abyss of barbarism. The instruments of colonial power rely on barbaric, brutal violence and intimidation, and the end result is the degradation of Europe itself. Hence Césaire can only scream: "Europe is indefensible." Europe is also dependent. Anticipating Fanon's famous proposition that "Europe is literally the creation of the Third World," Césaire reveals, over and over again, that the colonizers' sense of superiority, their sense of mission as the world's civilizers, depends on turning the Other into a barbarian.[2] The Africans, the Indians, the Asians cannot possess civilization or a culture equal to that of the imperialists, or the latter have no purpose, no justification for the exploitation and domination of the rest of the world. The colonial encounter, in other words, requires a reinvention of the colonized, the deliberate destruction of the past—what Césaire calls "thingification." *Discourse*, then, has a double-edged meaning: it is Césaire's discourse on the material and spiritual havoc created by colonialism, and it is a critique of colonial discourse. Anticipating the explosion of work we now call "postcolonial studies," Césaire's critique of figures such as Dominique O. Mannoni, Roger Caillois, Ernest Renan, Yves Florenne, and Jules Romains, among others, reveals how the circulation of colonial ideology—an ideology of racial and cultural hierarchy—is as essential to colonial rule as police and corvée labor.

Surprisingly, few assessments of postcolonial criticism pay much attention to *Discourse*, besides mentioning it in a litany of "pioneering" works without bothering to elaborate on its contents. Robert Young's *White Mythologies: Writing History and the West* (1990) dates the origins of postcolonial studies to Fanon's *Wretched of the Earth*, despite the fact that some of the arguments in Fanon were already present in *Discourse*.[3] On the other hand, literary critics tend to skip over *Discourse* or dismiss it as an anomaly born of Césaire's eleven-year stint as a member of the Communist Party of Martinique. It has been read in terms of whether it conforms to or breaks from "Marxist orthodoxy."[4] I want to suggest that *Discourse* made some critical contributions to our thinking about colonialism, fascism, and revolution. First, its recasting of the history of Western Civilization helps us locate the origins of fascism within colonialism itself; hence, within the very traditions of humanism, critics believed fascism threatened. Second, Césaire was neither confused about Marxism nor masquerading as a Marxist when he wrote *Discourse*. On the contrary, he was attempting to revise Marx, along the lines of his predecessors such as W.E.B. Du Bois and M.N. Roy, by suggesting that the anticolonial struggle supersedes the proletarian revolution as the fundamental historical movement of the period. The implications are enormous: the coming revolution was not posed in terms of capitalism versus socialism (the very last paragraph notwithstanding, but we shall return to this later), but in terms of the complete and total overthrow of a racist, colonialist system that would open the way to imagine a whole new world.

What such a world might look like is never spelled out, but that brings me to the final point about *Discourse*: it should be read as a surrealist text, perhaps even an unintended synthesis of Césaire's understanding of poetry (via Rimbaud) as revolt and his re-vision of historical materialism. For all of his Marxist criticism and Negritudian assertion, Césaire's text plumbs the depths of one's unconscious so that colonialism might be comprehended throughout the entire being. It is full of flares, full of anger, full of humor. It is not a solution or a strategy or a manual or a little red book with pithy quotes. It is a dancing flame in a bonfire.

Aimé Césaire's credentials as colonial critic are impeccable. He was born on June 26, 1913 in the small town of Basse-Pointe, Martinique where he, along with five siblings, were raised by a mother who was a dressmaker, and a father who held a post as the local tax inspector. Although their father was well educated and they shared the cultural sensibilities of the petit bourgeois, the Césaires nonetheless lived close to the edge of rural poverty. Aimé turned out to be a brilliant, precocious student and, at age eleven, was admitted to the Lycée Schoelcher in Fort-de-France. There he met Léon-Gontran Damas from Guiana, one of his childhood soccer-mates (who would go on to collaborate with Césaire and Senegalese poet Léopold Sédar Senghor in launching the Negritude movement). Césaire graduated from the Lycée in 1931 and took prizes in French, Latin, English, and history. Unlike many of his colleagues, he could not wait to leave home for the mother country—France. "I was not at ease in the Antillean world," he recalled. That would change during his eight-year stay in Paris.[5]

Once settled in Paris, he enrolled at the Lycée Louis-le-Grand to prepare for the grueling entrance exams to get into the Ecole Normale Supérieure. There he met a number of like-minded intellectuals, most notably Senghor. Meeting Senghor, and another Senegalese intellectual, Ousman Soce, inspired in Césaire an interest in Africa, and their collaborations eventually gave birth to the concept of Negritude. There were other black diasporic intellectual circles in Paris at the time, notably the group surrounding the Nardal sisters of Martinique (Paulette, Jane, and Andrée), who ran a salon out of which came *La Revue du monde noir*, edited by Paulette Nardal and Léo Sajous. Another circle of Martinican students, consisting mainly of Etienne Léro, René Ménil, J.M. Monnerot, and Pierre and Simone Yoyotte, joined together to declare their commitment to surrealism and communist revolution. In their one and only issue of *Légitime Défense*, published in 1932, they excoriated the French-speaking black bourgeoisie, attacked the servility of most West Indian literature, celebrated several black U.S. writers like Langston Hughes and Claude McKay, and denounced racism (paying special attention to the Scottsboro case). Césaire knew about the Nardal sisters' salon but found it entirely "too bourgeois" for his tastes. And though he had read *Légitime Défense*, he considered the group too assimilated: "There was nothing to distinguish them either from the French surrealists or the French Communists. In other words, their poems were colorless."[6]

Césaire, Senghor, Léon Damas, and others, were part of a different intellectual circle that centered around a journal called *L'Etudiant noir*. In its March 1935 issue, Césaire published a passionate tract against assimilation, in which he first coined the term "Negritude." It is more than ironic that at the moment Césaire's piece appeared, he was hard at work absorbing as much French and European humanities as possible in preparation for his entrance exams for the Ecole Normale Supérieure. The exams took their toll, for sure, though the psychic and emotional costs of having to imbibe the very culture Césaire publicly rejected must have exacerbated an already exhausting regimen. After completing his exams during the summer of 1935, he took a short vacation in Yugoslavia with a fellow student. While visiting the Adriatic coast, Césaire was overcome with memories of home after seeing a small island from a distance. Moved, he stayed up half the night working on a long poem about the Martinique of his youth—the land, the people, the majesty of the place. The next morning when he inquired about the little island, he was told it was called Martinska. A magical chance encounter, to say the least; the words he penned that moonlit night were the beginnings of what would subsequently become his most famous poem of all: *Cahier d'un retour au pays natal* (*Notebook of a Return to My Native Land*). The next summer he did return to Martinique, but was greeted by an even greater sense of alienation. He returned to France to complete his thesis on African-American writers of the Harlem Renaissance and their representations of the South, and then, on July 10, 1937, married Suzanne Roussy, a fellow Martinican student with whom he had worked on *L'Etudiant noir.*[7]

The couple returned to Martinique in 1939 and began teaching in Fort-de-France. Joining forces with René Ménil, Lucie Thésee, Aristide Maugée, Georges Gratiant, and others, they launched a journal called *Tropiques*. The appearance of *Tropiques* coincided with the fall of France to the fascist Vichy regime, which consequently put the colonies of Martinique, Guadeloupe, and Guiana under Vichy rule. The effect was startling; any illusions Césaire and his comrades might have harbored about colorblind French brotherhood were shattered when thousands of French sailors arrived on the island. Their racism was blatant and direct. As literary critic A. James Arnold observed, "The insensitivity of this military regime also made it difficult for Martinicans to ignore the fact that they were a colony like any other, a conclusion that the official policy of assimilation had masked somewhat. These conditions contributed to radicalizing Césaire and his friends, preparing them for a more anticolonialist posture at the end of the war."[8] The official policy of the regime to censor *Tropiques* and interdict the publication when it was deemed subversive also hastened the group's radicalization. In a notorious letter dated May 10, 1943, Martinique's Chief of Information Services, Captain Bayle, justified interdicting *Tropiques* for being "a revolutionary review that is racial and sectarian." Bayle accused the editors of poisoning the spirit of society, sowing hatred and ruining the morale of the country. Two days later, the editors penned a brilliant polemical response:

> To Lieutenant de Vaisseau Bayle:
>
> Sir, We have received your indictment of *Tropiques*.
>
> "Racists," "sectarians," "revolutionaries," "ingrates and traitors to the country," "poisoners of souls," none of these epithets really offends us. "Poisoners of Souls," like Racine, . . . "Ingrates and traitors to our good Country," like Zola, . . . "Revolutionaries," like the Hugo of "Châtiments." "Sectarians," passionately, like Rimbaud and Lautréamont. Racists, yes. Of the racism of Toussaint L'Ouverture, of Claude McKay and Langston Hughes against that of Drumont and Hitler. As to the rest of it, don't expect us to plead our case, or to launch into vain recriminations, or discussion. We do not speak the same language.
>
> Signed: Aimé Césaire, Suzanne Césaire, Georges Gratiant, Aristide Maugée, René Ménil, Lucie Thésée.[9]

But in order for *Tropiques* to survive, they had to camouflage their boldness, passing it off as a journal of West Indian folklore. Yet, despite the repressions and the ruses, *Tropiques* survived the war as one of the most important and radical surrealist publications in the world. Lasting from 1941 to 1945, the essays and poems it published (by the Césaires, René Ménil, and others) reveal the evolution of a sophisticated anticolonial stance, as well as a vision of a postcolonial future. Theirs was a vision of freedom that drew on Modernism and a deep appreciation for pre-colonial African modes of thought and practice; it drew on Surrealism as the strategy of revolution of the mind and Marxism as revolution of the productive forces. It was an effort to carve out a position independent of all of these forces, a kind of wedding of Negritude, Marxism, and surrealism, and their collective efforts would have a profound impact on international surrealism, in general, and on André Breton, in particular. *Tropiques* also published Breton, as well as texts by Pierre Mabille, Benjamin Peret, and other surrealists.[10] In fact, it is not too much to proclaim Suzanne Césaire as one of surrealism's most original theorists. Unlike critics who boxed surrealism into narrow "avant garde" tendencies such as futurism or cubism, Suzanne Césaire linked it to broader movements such as Romanticism, socialism, and Negritude. Surrealism, she argued, was not an ideology as such but a state of mind, a "permanent readiness for the Marvelous." In a 1941 issue of *Tropiques*, she imagined new possibilities in terms that were foreign to Marxists; she called on readers to embrace "the domain of the strange, the marvelous and the fantastic, a domain scorned by people of certain inclinations. Here is the freed image, dazzling and beautiful, with a beauty that could not be more unexpected and overwhelming. Here are the poet, the painter, and the artist, presiding over the metamorphoses and the inversions of the world under the sign of hallucination and madness."[11] And yet, when she speaks of the domain of the Marvelous, she has her sights on the chains of colonial domination, never forgetting the crushing reality of everyday life in Martinique and the rest of the world. In "Surrealism and Us: 1943," she writes with a boldness and clarity that would come to characterize her husband's *Discourse on Colonialism*:

> Thus, far from contradicting, diluting, or diverting our revolutionary attitude toward life, surrealism strengthens it. It nourishes an impatient strength within us, endlessly reinforcing the massive army of refusals.

And I am also thinking of tomorrow.

Millions of black hands will fling their terror across the furious skies of world war. Freed from a long benumbing slumber, the most disinherited of all peoples will rise up from plains of ashes.

Our surrealism will supply this rising people with a punch from its very depths. Our surrealism will enable us to finally transcend the sordid dichotomies of the present: whites/Blacks, Europeans/Africans, civilized/savages—at last rediscovering the magic power of the *mahoulis*, drawn directly from living sources. Colonial idiocy will be purified in the welder's blue flame. We shall recover our value as metal, our cutting edge of steel, our unprecedented communions.[12]

Although the influence of surrealism on Aimé Césaire has been called into question recently, the question of his surrealism is usually posed in terms of André Breton's influence on Césaire. Surrealism in this context is treated as "European thought," and like Marxism, considered foreign to non-European traditions. But this sort of "diffusionist" interpretation leaves no room for the Césaires (both Aimé and Suzanne) to be innovators of surrealism, to have introduced fresh ideas to Breton and his colleagues. I want to suggest that the Césaires not only embraced surrealism—independently of the Paris Group, I might add—but opened new vistas and contributed enormously to theorizing the "domain of the Marvelous."[13]

Aimé Césaire, after all, has never denied his surrealist leanings. As he explains in the interview appended here: "Surrealism provided me with what I had been confusedly searching for. I have accepted it joyfully because in it I have found more of a confirmation than a revelation." Surrealism, he explained, helped him to summon up powerful unconscious forces. "This, for me, was a call to Africa. I said to myself: it's true that superficially we are

French, we bear the marks of French customs; we have been branded by Cartesian philosophy, by French rhetoric; but if we break with all that, if we plumb the depths, then what we will find is fundamentally black." And, in another interview with Jacqueline Leiner, he was even more enthusiastic about Breton's role: "Breton brought us boldness, he helped us take a strong stand. He cut short our hesitations and research. I realized that the majority of the problems I encountered had already been resolved by Breton and surrealism. I would say that my meeting with Breton was confirmation of what I had arrived at on my own. This saved us time, let us go quicker, further. The encounter was extraordinary."[14] Furthermore, even as a communist deputy in the later 1940s, Césaire continued to publish poetry for surrealist publications such as *Le Surrealism en 1947*, an exhibit catalogue edited by André Breton and Marcel Duchamp. His surrealist imagery is undeniable in two poetry collections from that era, *Les Armes miraculeuses* (Miraculous Weapons) in 1944 and *Soleil cou coupé* (Beheaded Sun) in 1948.[15]

Césaire's essay, "Poetry and Cognition," which he delivered during his seven-month visit to Haiti in 1944, and which appeared in *Tropiques* the following year, represents one of his most systematic statements on the revolutionary nature of poetry. Opening with the simple but provocative proposition that "Poetic knowledge is born in the great silence of scientific knowledge," he then attempts to demonstrate why poetry is the only way to achieve the kind of knowledge we need to move beyond the world's crises. Césaire's embrace of poetry as a method of achieving clairvoyance, of obtaining the knowledge we need to move forward, is crucial for understanding *Discourse*, which appears just five years later. If we think of *Discourse* as a kind of historical prose poem against the realities of colonialism, then perhaps we should heed Césaire's point that "What presides over the poem is not the most lucid intelligence, the sharpest sensibility or the subtlest feelings, but experience as a whole." This means everything, every history, every future, every dream, every life form, from plant to animal, every creative impulse—is plumbed from the depths of the unconscious. If poetry is, indeed, a powerful source of knowledge and revolt, one might expect Césaire to employ it as *Discourse*'s sharpest weapon. And I think most readers will agree that those passages which sing, that sound the war drums, that explode spontaneously, are the most powerful sections of the essay. But those readers who are expecting a systematic critique replete with hypotheses, sufficient evidence, topic sentences, and bullet points, are bound for disappointment. Consider Césaire's third proposition regarding poetic knowledge: "Poetic knowledge is that in which man spatters the object with all of his mobilized riches."[16]

Surrealism is also important to the formation of *Discourse* because, like the movements that gave rise to Pan-Africanism and Negritude, it has its own independent anticolonial roots. I am not suggesting that Césaire's critique of colonialism necessarily derived from the surrealists; rather, I want to suggest that the mutual attraction engendered between Césaire (and many other black intellectuals at the time) and the surrealists can be partly explained by affinities in their position toward Empire. Up until the mid-1920s, the European surrealists were largely cultural iconoclasts who made radical pronouncements but displayed little interest in social revolution. But that would change in 1925, when the Paris Surrealist Group and the extreme left of the French Communist Party were drawn together by their support of Abd-el-Krim, leader of the Rif uprising against French colonialism in Morocco. They actively called for the overthrow of French colonial rule. That same year, in an "Open Letter" to Paul Claudel, writer and French ambassador to Japan, the Paris group announced: "We profoundly hope that revolutions, wars, colonial insurrections, will annihilate this Western civilization whose vermin you defend even in the Orient." Seven years later, the Paris group produced its most militant statement on the colonial question to date. Titled "Murderous Humanitarianism" (1932) and drafted mainly by René Crevel and signed by André Breton, Paul Eluard, Benjamin Peret, Yves Tanguy, and the Martinican surrealists Pierre Yoyotte and J.M. Monnerot, the document is a relentless attack on colonialism, capitalism, the clergy, the black bourgeoisie, and hypocritical liberals. They argue that the very humanism upon which the modern West was built also justified slavery, colonialism, and genocide. And they called for action, noting, "we Surrealists pronounced ourselves in favor of changing the imperialist war, in its chronic and colonial form, into a civil war. Thus we placed our energies at the disposal of the revolution, of the proletariat and its struggles, and defined our attitude towards the colonial problem, and hence towards the color question."[17]

While "Murderous Humanitarianism" certainly resonates with Césaire's critique, he had less faith in the proletariat—the European proletariat, that is—than those who signed this document. Moreover, as a product of the period following the Second World War, *Discourse* goes one step further by drawing a direct link between the logic of colonialism and the rise of fascism. Césaire provocatively points out that Europeans tolerated "Nazism before it was inflicted on them, that they absolved it, shut their eyes to it, legitimized it, because, until then, it had been applied only to non-European peoples; that they have cultivated that Nazism, that they are responsible for it, and that before engulfing the whole edifice of Western,

Christian civilization in its reddened waters, it oozes, seeps, and trickles from every crack." So the real crime of fascism was the application to white people of colonial procedures "which until then had been reserved exclusively for the Arabs of Algeria, the 'coolies' of India, and the 'niggers' of Africa." (p. 36) Here we must situate Césaire within a larger context of radical black intellectuals who had come to the same conclusions before the publication of *Discourse*. As Cedric Robinson argues, a group of radical black intellectuals, including W.E.B. Du Bois, C.L.R. James, George Padmore, and Oliver Cox, understood fascism not as some aberration from the march of progress, an unexpected right-wing turn, but a logical development of Western Civilization itself. They viewed fascism as a blood relative of slavery and imperialism, global systems rooted not only in capitalist political economy but racist ideologies that were already in place at the dawn of modernity. As early as 1936, Ralph Bunche, then a radical political science professor at Howard University, suggested that imperialism gave birth to fascism. "The doctrine of Fascism," wrote Bunche, "with its extreme jingoism, its exaggerated exaltation of the state and its comic-opera glorification of race, has given a new and greater impetus to the policy of world imperialism which had conquered and subjected to systematic and ruthless exploitation virtually all of the darker populations of the earth." Du Bois made some of the clearest statements to this effect: "I knew that Hitler and Mussolini were fighting communism, and using race prejudice to make some white people rich and all colored people poor. But it was not until later that I realized that the colonialism of Great Britain and France had exactly the same object and methods as the fascists and the Nazis were trying clearly to use." Later, in *The World and Africa* (1947), he writes: "There was no Nazi atrocity—concentration camps, wholesale maiming and mur-

der, defilement of women or ghastly blasphemy of childhood—
which Christian civilization or Europe had not long been practicing
against colored folk in all parts of the world in the name of and for
the defense of a Superior Race born to rule the world."[18]

The very idea that there was a superior race lay at the heart of
the matter, and this is why elements of *Discourse* also drew on
Negritude's impulse to recover the history of Africa's accomplish-
ments. Taking his cue from Leo Frobenius's injunction that the
"idea of the barbaric Negro is a European invention,"[19] Césaire sets
out to prove that the colonial mission to "civilize" the primitive is
just a smoke screen. If anything, colonialism results in the massive
destruction of whole societies—societies that not only function at
a high level of sophistication and complexity, but that might offer
the West valuable lessons about how we might live together and
remake the modern world. Indeed, Césaire's insistence that pre-colonial African and Asian cultures "were not only ante-capitalist . . . but
also anti-capitalist," anticipated romantic claims advanced by African
nationalist leaders such as Julius Nyerere, Kenneth Kaunda, and
Senghor himself, that modern Africa can establish socialism on the
basis of pre-colonial village life.

Discourse was not the first place Césaire made the case for the
barbaric West following the path of the civilized African. In his Introduction to Victor Schoelcher's *Esclavage et colonisation*, he wrote:

> The men they took away knew how to build houses, govern empires,
> erect cities, cultivate fields, mine for metals, weave cotton, forge steel.

> Their religion had its own beauty, based on mystical connections
> with the founder of the city. Their customs were pleasing, built on
> unity, kindness, respect for age.

No coercion, only mutual assistance, the joy of living, a free acceptance of discipline.

Order—Earnestness—Poetry and Freedom.[20]

Reading this passage, and the book itself, deeply affected one of Césaire's brightest students, named Frantz Fanon. It was a revelation for him to discover cities in Africa and "accounts of learned blacks." "All of that," he noted in *Black Skin, White Masks* (1952), "exhumed from the past, spread with its insides out, made it possible for me to find a valid historical place. The white man was wrong, I was not a primitive, not even a half-man, I belonged to a race that had already been working in gold and silver two thousand years ago."[21]

Negritude turned out to be a miraculous weapon in the struggle to overthrow the "barbaric Negro." As Cedric Robinson points out in *Black Marxism: The Making of the Black Radical Tradition*, this was no easy task, since the invention of the Negro—and by extension the fabrication of whiteness and all the racial boundary policing that came with it—required "immense expenditures of psychic and intellectual energies of the West." An entire generation of "enlightened" European scholars worked hard to wipe out the cultural and intellectual contributions of Egypt and Nubia from European history, to whiten the West in order to maintain the purity of the "European" race. They also stripped all of Africa of any semblance of "civilization," using the printed page to eradicate their history and thus reduce a whole continent and its progeny to little more than beasts of burden or brutish heathens. The result is the fabrication of Europe as a discrete, racially pure entity, solely responsible for modernity, on the one hand, and the fabrication of the Negro on the other.[22]

Yet, despite Césaire's construction of pre-colonial Africa as an aggregation of warm, communal societies, he never calls for a return. Unlike his old friend Senghor, Césaire's concept of Negritude is future-oriented and modern. His position in *Discourse* is unequivocal: "For us the problem is not to make a utopian and sterile attempt to repeat the past, but to go beyond. It is not a dead society that we want to revive. We leave that to those who go in for exoticism. . . . It is a new society that we must create, with the help of our brother slaves, a society rich with all the productive power of modern times, warm with all the fraternity of olden days."

Then comes the shocking next line:

"For some examples showing that this is possible, we can look to the Soviet Union."

By 1950, of course, Césaire had been a leader in the Communist Party of Martinique for about five years. On the Communist ticket, he was elected mayor of Fort-de-France as well as Deputy to the French National Assembly. Now, given everything he has written thus far, everything that he has lived, why would he hold up Stalinism circa 1950s as an exemplar of the new society? Why would a great poet and major voice of surrealism and Negritude suddenly join the Communist Party? Actually, once we consider the context of the postwar world, his decision is not shocking at all. First, remember that Communist parties worldwide, especially in Europe, were at their height immediately after the war, and Joe Stalin spent the war years as an ally of liberal democracy. Second, several leading writers and artists committed to radical social change, particularly in the Caribbean and Latin America, became Communists—including Césaire's friends, Jacques Romain, Nicolas Guillén, and René Depestre. Third, Césaire, who was reluctant to become involved in politics, discovered early on that he could be effective.

Almost as soon as he was elected, Césaire set out to change the status of Martinique, Guadeloupe, Guiana, and Réunion from colonies to "departments" within the French Republic. Departmentalization, he insisted, would put these areas on an equal footing with departments in metropolitan France. Césaire's eloquent and passionate arguments led to a law in 1946 resulting in departmentalization. However, his dream that assimilation of the old colonies into the republic would guarantee equal rights turned out to be a pipe dream. In the end, French officials were sent to the colonies in greater numbers, often displacing some of the local black Martinican bureaucrats. By the time he drafted the popularly known third edition of *Discourse* in 1955, he had become an outspoken critic of departmentalization.[23]

Thus, given Césaire's role as Communist leader, we should not be surprised by *Discourse*'s nod to the Soviet Union, or even the final closing lines of the text, in which he names proletarian revolution as our savior. What is jarring, however, is how incongruous these statements are in relation to the rest of the text. After demonstrating that Europe is a dying civilization, one on the verge of self-destruction (in which the chickens of colonial violence and tyranny have come home to roost while the white working class looks on in silent complicity), he proposes proletarian revolution as the final solution! Yet, throughout the book, he anticipates Fanon, implying that there is nothing worth saving in Europe, that the European working class has too often joined forces with the European bourgeoisie in their support of racism, imperialism, and colonialism, and that the uprisings of the colonized might point the way forward. Ultimately, *Discourse* is a challenge to, or revision of, Marxism; it draws on surrealism and the anti-rationalist ideas of Césaire's early poetry and explorations in Negritude. It is fairly unmaterialist in the way it cries out for new spiritual values to emerge out of the study of what colonialism sought to destroy.

Césaire's position vis-à-vis Marxism becomes even clearer less than one year after the third edition of *Discourse* appeared. In October 1956, Césaire pens his famous letter to Maurice Thorez, Secretary General of the French Communist Party, tendering his resignation from the party. Besides its stinging rebuke of Stalinism, the heart of the letter dealt with the colonial question—not just the Party's policies toward the colonies but the colonial relationship between the metropolitan and the Martinican Communist Parties. Arguing that people of color need to exercise self-determination, he warned against treating the "colonial question . . . as a subsidiary part of some more important global matter." Racism, in other words, cannot be subordinate to the class struggle. His letter is an even bolder, more direct assertion of third world unity than *Discourse*. Although he still identifies as a Marxist and is still open to alliances, he cautions that there "are no allies by divine right." If following the Communist Party "pillages our most vivifying friendships, breaks the bond that weds us to other West Indian islands, severs the tie that makes us Africa's child, then I say communism has served us ill in having us trade a living brotherhood for what seems to be the coldest of all chill abstractions." More important, Césaire's investment in a third-world revolt paving the way for a new society certainly anticipates Fanon. He had practically given up on Europe and the old humanism and its claims of universality, opting instead to re-define the "universal" in a way that did not privilege Europe. Césaire explains, "I'm not going to confine myself to some narrow particularism. But I don't intend either to become lost in a disembodied universalism . . . . I have a different idea of a universal. It is a universal rich with all that is particular, rich with all the particulars there are, the deepening of each particular, the coexistence of them all."[24]

What Césaire articulates in *Discourse*, and more explicitly in his letter to Thorez, distills the spirit that swept through African intellectual circles in the age of decolonization. This pervasive spirit was what Negritude was all about then; it was never a simple matter of racial essentialism. Critic, scholar, and filmmaker Manthia Diawara beautifully captures the atmosphere of the era and, implicitly, what these radical critiques of the colonial order, such as *Discourse on Colonialism,* meant to a new generation: "The idea that Negritude was bigger even than Africa, that we were part of an international moment which held the promise of universal emancipation, that our destiny coincided with the universal freedom of workers and colonized people worldwide—all this gave us a bigger and more important identity than the ones previously available to us through kinship, ethnicity, and race . . . . The awareness of our new historical mission freed us from what we regarded in those days as the archaic identities of our fathers and their religious entrapments; it freed us from race and banished our fear of the whiteness of French identity. To be labeled the saviors of humanity, when only recently we had been colonized and despised by the world, gave us a feeling of righteousness, which bred contempt for capitalism, racialism of all origins, and tribalism."[25]

In light of recent events—genocide in East Africa, the collapse of democracy throughout the continent, the isolation of Cuba, the overthrow of progressive movements throughout the so-called third world—some might argue that the moment of truth has already passed, that Césaire and Fanon's predictions proved false. We're facing an era where fools are calling for a renewal of colonialism, where descriptions of violence and instability draw on the very colonial language of "barbarism" and "backwardness" that Césaire critiques in these pages. But this is all a mystification; the fact is, while colonialism in its formal sense might have been dismantled, the colonial state has not. Many of the problems of democracy are products of the old colonial state whose primary difference is the presence of black faces. It has to do with the rise of a new ruling class—the class Fanon warned us about—who are content with mimicking the colonial masters, whether they are the old-school British or French officers, the new jack U.S. corporate rulers, or the Stalinists whose sympathy for the "backward" countries often mirrored the very colonial discourse Césaire exposes.

As the true radicals of postcolonial theory will tell you, we are hardly in a "postcolonial" moment. The official apparatus might have been removed, but the political, economic, and cultural links established by colonial domination still remain with some alterations. *Discourse* is less concerned with the specifics of political economy than with a way of thinking. The lesson here is that colonial domination required a whole way of thinking, a discourse in which everything that is advanced, good, and civilized is defined and measured in European terms. *Discourse* calls on the world to move forward as rapidly as possible, and yet calls for the overthrow of a master class's ideology of progress, one built on violence, destruction, genocide. Both Fanon and Césaire warn the colored world not to follow Europe's footsteps, and not to go back to the ancient way, but to carve out a new direction altogether. What we've been witnessing, however (and here I must include Césaire's own beloved Martinique, where he still holds forth as mayor of Fort-de-France) hardly reflects the imagination and vision captured in these brief pages. The same old political parties, the same armies, the same methods of labor exploitation, the same education, the same tactics of incarceration, exiling, snuffing out artists and intellectuals who dare to imagine a radically different way of living, who dare to invent the marvelous before our very eyes.

In the end, *Discourse* was never intended to be a road map or a blueprint for revolution. It is poetry and therefore revolt. It is an act of insurrection, drawn from Césaire's own miraculous weapons, molded and shaped by his work with *Tropiques* and its challenge to the Vichy regime; by his imbibing of European culture and his sense of alienation from both France and his native land. It is a rising, a blow to the master who appears as owner and ruler, teacher and comrade. It is revolutionary graffiti painted in bold strokes across the great texts of Western Civilization; it is a hand grenade tossed with deadly accuracy, clearing the field so that we might write a new history with what's left standing. *Discourse* is hardly a dead document about a dead order. If anything, it is a call for us to plumb the depths of the imagination for a different way forward. Just as Césaire drew on Lautréamont's *Chants de Maldoror* to illuminate the cannibalistic nature of capitalism and the power of poetic knowledge, *Discourse* offers new insights into the consequences of colonialism and a model for dreaming a way out of our postcolonial predicament. While we still need to overthrow all vestiges of the old colonial order, destroying the old is just half the battle.

DISCOURSE ON COLONIALISM

Aimé Césaire

Translated by Joan Pinkham

DISCOURSE ON COLONIALISM

by Aimé Césaire

A civilization that proves incapable of solving the problems it creates is a decadent civilization.

A civilization that chooses to close its eyes to its most crucial problems is a stricken civilization.

A civilization that uses its principles for trickery and deceit is a dying civilization.

The fact is that the so-called European civilization—"Western" civilization—as it has been shaped by two centuries of bourgeois rule, is incapable of solving the two major problems to which its existence has given rise: the problem of the proletariat and the colonial problem; that Europe is unable to justify itself either before the bar of "reason" or before the bar of "conscience"; and that, increasingly, it takes refuge in a hypocrisy which is all the more odious because it is less and less likely to deceive.

Europe is indefensible.

Apparently that is what the American strategists are whispering to each other.

That in itself is not serious.

What is serious is that "Europe" is morally, spiritually indefensible.

And today the indictment is brought against it not by the European masses alone, but on a world scale, by tens and tens of millions of men who, from the depths of slavery, set themselves up as judges.

The colonialists may kill in Indochina, torture in Madagascar, imprison in Black Africa, crack down in the West Indies. Henceforth the colonized know that they have an advantage over them. They know that their temporary "masters" are lying.

Therefore that their masters are weak.

And since I have been asked to speak about colonization and civilization, let us go straight to the principal lie that is the source of all the others.

Colonization and civilization?

In dealing with this subject, the commonest curse is to be the dupe in good faith of a collective hypocrisy that cleverly misrepresents problems, the better to legitimize the hateful solutions provided for them.

In other words, the essential thing here is to see clearly, to think clearly—that is, dangerously—and to answer clearly the innocent first question: what, fundamentally, is colonization? To agree on what it is not: neither evangelization, nor a philanthropic enterprise, nor a desire to push back the frontiers of ignorance, disease, and tyranny, nor a project undertaken for the greater glory of God, nor an attempt to extend the rule of law. To admit once and for all, without flinching at the consequences, that the decisive actors here are the adventurer and the pirate, the wholesale grocer and the ship owner, the gold digger and the merchant, appetite and force, and behind them, the baleful projected shadow of a form of civilization which, at a certain point in its history, finds itself obliged, for internal reasons, to extend to a world scale the competition of its antagonistic economies.

Pursuing my analysis, I find that hypocrisy is of recent date; that neither Cortéz discovering Mexico from the top of the great teocalli, nor Pizzaro before Cuzco (much less Marco Polo before Cambuluc), claims that he is the harbinger of a superior order; that they kill; that they plunder; that they have helmets, lances, cupidities; that the slavering apologists came later; that the chief culprit in this domain is Christian pedantry, which laid down the dishonest equations *Christianity = civilization, paganism = savagery,* from which there could not but ensue abominable colonialist and racist consequences, whose victims were to be the Indians, the Yellow peoples, and the Negroes.

That being settled, I admit that it is a good thing to place different civilizations in contact with each other; that it is an excellent thing to blend different worlds; that whatever its own particular genius may be, a civilization that withdraws into itself atrophies; that for civilizations, exchange is oxygen; that the great good fortune of Europe is to have been a crossroads, and that because it was the locus of all ideas, the receptacle of all philosophies, the meeting place of all sentiments, it was the best center for the redistribution of energy.

But then I ask the following question: has colonization really *placed civilizations in contact?* Or, if you prefer, of all the ways of *establishing contact,* was it the best?

I answer *no.*

And I say that between *colonization* and *civilization* there is an infinite distance; that out of all the colonial expeditions that have been undertaken, out of all the colonial statutes that have been drawn up, out of all the memoranda that have been dispatched by all the ministries, there could not come a single human value.

First we must study how colonization works to *decivilize* the colonizer, to *brutalize* him in the true sense of the word, to degrade him, to awaken him to buried instincts, to covetousness, violence, race hatred, and moral relativism; and we must show that each time a head is cut off or an eye put out in Vietnam and in France they accept the fact, each time a little girl is raped and in France they accept the fact, each time a Madagascan is tortured and in France they accept the fact, civilization acquires another dead weight, a universal regression takes place, a gangrene sets in, a center of infection begins to spread; and that at the end of all these treaties that have been violated, all these lies that have been propagated, all these punitive expeditions that have been tolerated, all these prisoners who have been tied up and "interrogated," all these patriots who have been tortured, at the end of all the racial pride that has been encouraged, all the boastfulness that has been displayed, a

35

poison has been distilled into the veins of Europe and, slowly but surely, the continent proceeds toward *savagery.*

And then one fine day the bourgeoisie is awakened by a terrific boomerang effect: the gestapos are busy, the prisons fill up, the torturers standing around the racks invent, refine, discuss.

People are surprised, they become indignant. They say: "How strange! But never mind—it's Nazism, it will pass!" And they wait, and they hope; and they hide the truth from themselves, that it is barbarism, the supreme barbarism, the crowning barbarism that sums up all the daily barbarisms; that it is Nazism, yes, but that before they were its victims, they were its accomplices; that they tolerated that Nazism before it was inflicted on them, that they absolved it, shut their eyes to it, legitimized it, because, until then, it had been applied only to non-European peoples; that they cultivated that Nazism, that they are responsible for it, and that before engulfing the whole edifice of Western, Christian civilization in its reddened waters, it oozes, seeps, and trickles from every crack.

Yes, it would be worthwhile to study clinically, in detail, the steps taken by Hitler and Hitlerism and to reveal to the very distinguished, very humanistic, very Christian bourgeois of the twentieth century that without his being aware of it, he has a Hitler inside him, that Hitler *inhabits* him, that Hitler is his *demon,* that if he rails against him, he is being inconsistent and that, at bottom, what he cannot forgive Hitler for is not *the crime* in itself, *the crime against man,* it is not *the humiliation of man as such,* it is the crime against the white man, the humiliation of the white man, and the fact that he applied to Europe colonialist procedures which until then had been reserved exclusively for the Arabs of Algeria, the "coolies" of India, and the "niggers" of Africa.

And that is the great thing I hold against pseudo-humanism: that for too long it has diminished the rights of man, that its concept of those rights has been—and still is—narrow and fragmentary, incomplete and biased and, all things considered, sordidly racist.

I have talked a good deal about Hitler. Because he deserves it: he makes it possible to see things on a large scale and to grasp the fact that capitalist society, at its present stage, is incapable of establishing a concept of the rights of all men, just as it has proved incapable of establishing a system of individual ethics. Whether one likes it or not, at the end of the blind alley that is Europe, I mean the Europe of Adenauer, Schuman, Bidault, and a few others, there is Hitler. At the end of capitalism, which is eager to outlive its day, there is Hitler. At the end of formal humanism and philosophic renunciation, there is Hitler.

And this being so, I cannot help thinking of one of his statements: "We aspire not to equality but to domination. The country of a foreign race must become once again a country of serfs, of agricultural laborers, or industrial workers. It is not a question of eliminating the inequalities among men but of widening them and making them into a law."

That rings clear, haughty, and brutal, and plants us squarely in the middle of howling savagery. But let us come down a step.

Who is speaking? I am ashamed to say it: it is the Western *humanist*, the "idealist" philosopher. That his name is Renan is an accident. That the passage is taken from a book entitled *La Réforme intellectuelle et morale*, that it was written in France just after a war which France had represented as a war of right against might, tells us a great deal about bourgeois morals.

The regeneration of the inferior or degenerate races by the superior races is part of the providential order of things for humanity. With us, the common man is nearly always a déclassé nobleman, his heavy hand is better suited to handling the sword than the menial tool. Rather than work, he chooses to fight, that is, he returns to his first estate. *Regere imperio populos,* that is our vocation. Pour forth this all-consuming activity onto countries which, like China, are crying aloud for foreign conquest. Turn the adventurers who disturb European society into a *ver sacrum,* a horde like those of the Franks, the Lombards, or the Normans, and every man will be in his right role. Nature has made a race of workers, the Chinese race, who have wonderful manual dexterity and almost no sense of honor; govern them with justice, levying from them, in return for the blessing of such a government, an ample allowance for the conquering race, and they will be satisfied; a race of tillers of the soil, the Negro; treat him with kindness and humanity, and all will be as it should; a race of masters and soldiers, the European race. Reduce this noble race to working in the *ergastulum* like Negroes and Chinese, and they rebel. In Europe, every rebel is, more or less, a soldier who has missed his calling, a creature made for the heroic life, before whom you are setting *a task that is contrary to his race*, a poor worker, too good a soldier. But the life at which our workers rebel would make a Chinese or a fellah happy, as they are not military creatures in the least. *Let each one do what he is made for, and all will be well.*

Hitler? Rosenberg? No, Renan.

But let us come down one step further. And it is the long-winded politician. Who protests? No one, so far as I know, when M. Albert Sarraut, the former governor-general of Indochina, holding forth to the students at the Ecole Coloniale, teaches them that it would be puerile to object to the European colonial enterprises in the name of "an alleged right to possess the land one occupies, and some sort of right to remain in fierce isolation, which would leave unutilized resources to lie forever idle in the hands of incompetents."

And who is roused to indignation when a certain Rev. Barde assures us that if the goods of this world "remained divided up indefinitely, as they would be without colonization, they would answer neither the purposes of God nor the just demands of the human collectivity"?

Since, as his fellow Christian, the Rev. Muller, declares: "Humanity must not, cannot allow the incompetence, negligence, and laziness of the uncivilized peoples to leave idle indefinitely the wealth which God has confided to them, charging them to make it serve the good of all."

No one.

I mean not one established writer, not one academic, not one preacher, not one crusader for the right and for religion, not one "defender of the human person."

And yet, through the mouths of the Sarrauts and the Bardes, the Mullers and the Renans, through the mouths of all those who considered—and consider—it lawful to apply to non-European peoples "a kind of expropriation for public purposes" for the benefit of nations that were stronger and better equipped, it was already Hitler speaking!

What am I driving at? At this idea: that no one colonizes innocently, that no one colonizes with impunity either; that a nation which colonizes, that a civilization which justifies colonization—and therefore force—is already a sick civilization, a civilization which is morally diseased, which irresistibly, progressing from one consequence to another, one denial to another, calls for its Hitler, I mean its punishment.

Colonization: bridgehead in a campaign to civilize barbarism, from which there may emerge at any moment the negation of civilization, pure and simple.

Elsewhere I have cited at length a few incidents culled from the history of colonial expeditions.

Unfortunately, this did not find favor with everyone. It seems that I was pulling old skeletons out of the closet. Indeed!

Was there no point in quoting Colonel de Montagnac, one of the conquerors of Algeria: "In order to banish the thoughts that sometimes besiege me, I have some heads cut off, not the heads of artichokes but the heads of men."

Would it have been more advisable to refuse the floor to Count d'Hérisson: "It is true that we are bringing back a whole barrelful of ears collected, pair by pair, from prisoners, friendly or enemy."

Should I have denied Saint-Arnaud the right to profess his barbarous faith: "We lay waste, we burn, we plunder, we destroy the houses and the trees."

Should I have prevented Marshal Bugeaud from systematizing all that in a daring theory and invoking the precedent of famous ancestors: "We must have a great invasion of Africa, like the invasions of the Franks and the Goths."

Lastly, should I have cast back into the shadows of oblivion the memorable feat of arms of General Gérard and kept silent about the capture of Ambike, a city which, to tell the truth, had never dreamed of defending itself: "The native riflemen had orders to kill only the men, but no one restrained them; intoxicated by the smell of blood, they spared not one woman, not one child. . . . At the end of the afternoon, the heat caused a light mist to arise: it was the blood of the five thousand victims, the ghost of the city, evaporating in the setting sun."

Yes or no, are these things true? And the sadistic pleasures, the nameless delights that send voluptuous shivers and quivers through Loti's carcass when he focuses his field glasses on a good massacre of the Annamese? True or not true? And if these things are true, as no one can deny, will it be said, in order to minimize them, that these corpses don't prove anything?

For my part, if I have recalled a few details of these hideous butcheries, it is by no means because I take a morbid delight in them, but because I think that these heads of men, these collections of ears, these burned houses, these Gothic invasions, this steaming blood, these cities that evaporate at the edge of the sword, are not to be so easily disposed of. They prove that colonization, I repeat, dehumanizes even the most civilized man; that colonial activity, colonial enterprise, colonial conquest, which is based on contempt for the native and justified by that contempt, inevitably tends to change him who undertakes it; that the colonizer, who in order to ease his conscience gets into the habit of seeing the other man as *an animal,* accustoms himself to treating him like an animal, and tends objectively to transform *himself* into an animal. It is this result, this boomerang effect of colonization that I wanted to point out.

Unfair? No. There was a time when these same facts were a source of pride, and when, sure of the morrow, people did not mince words. One last quotation; it is from a certain Carl Siger, author of an *Essai sur la colonisation* (Paris, 1907):

> The new countries offer a vast field for individual, violent activities which, in the metropolitan countries, would run up against certain prejudices, against a sober and orderly conception of life, and which, in the colonies, have greater freedom to develop and, consequently, to affirm their worth. Thus to a certain extent the colonies

can serve as a safety valve for modern society. Even if this were their only value, it would be immense.

Truly, there are sins for which no one has the power to make amends and which can never be fully expiated.

But let us speak about the colonized.

I see clearly what colonization has destroyed: the wonderful Indian civilizations—and neither Deterding nor Royal Dutch nor Standard Oil will ever console me for the Aztecs and the Incas.

I see clearly the civilizations, condemned to perish at a future date, into which it has introduced a principle of ruin: the South Sea Islands, Nigeria, Nyasaland. I see less clearly the contributions it has made.

Security? Culture? The rule of law? In the meantime, I look around and wherever there are colonizers and colonized face to face, I see force, brutality, cruelty, sadism, conflict, and, in a parody of education, the hasty manufacture of a few thousand subordinate functionaries, "boys," artisans, office clerks, and interpreters necessary for the smooth operation of business.

I spoke of contact.

Between colonizer and colonized there is room only for forced labor, intimidation, pressure, the police, taxation, theft, rape, compulsory crops, contempt, mistrust, arrogance, self-complacency, swinishness, brainless elites, degraded masses.

No human contact, but relations of domination and submission which turn the colonizing man into a classroom monitor, an army sergeant, a prison guard, a slave driver, and the indigenous man into an instrument of production.

My turn to state an equation: colonization = "thingification."

I hear the storm. They talk to me about progress, about "achievements," diseases cured, improved standards of living.

I am talking about societies drained of their essence, cultures trampled underfoot, institutions undermined, lands confiscated, religions smashed, magnificent artistic creations destroyed, extraordinary *possibilities* wiped out.

They throw facts at my head, statistics, mileages of roads, canals, and railroad tracks.

I am talking about thousands of men sacrificed to the Congo-Océan.[2] I am talking about those who, as I write this, are digging the harbor of Abidjan by hand. I am talking about millions of men torn from their gods, their land, their habits, their life—from life, from the dance, from wisdom.

I am talking about millions of men in whom fear has been cunningly instilled, who have been taught to have an inferiority complex, to tremble, kneel, despair, and behave like flunkeys.

They dazzle me with the tonnage of cotton or cocoa that has been exported, the acreage that has been planted with olive trees or grape-vines.

I am talking about natural *economies* that have been disrupted—harmonious and viable *economies* adapted to the indigenous population—about food crops destroyed, malnutrition permanently introduced, agricultural development oriented solely toward the benefit of the metropolitan countries; about the looting of products, the looting of raw materials.

They pride themselves on abuses eliminated.

I too talk about abuses, but what I say is that on the old ones—very real—they have superimposed others—very detestable. They talk to me about local tyrants brought to reason; but I note that in general the old tyrants get on very well with the new ones, and that there has been established between them, to the detriment of the people, a circuit of mutual services and complicity.

They talk to me about civilization, I talk about proletarianization and mystification.

For my part, I make a systematic defense of the non-European civilizations.

Every day that passes, every denial of justice, every beating by the police, every demand of the workers that is drowned in blood, every scandal that is hushed up, every punitive expedition, every police van, every gendarme and every militiaman, brings home to us the value of our old societies.

They were communal societies, never societies of the many for the few.

They were societies that were not only ante-capitalist, as has been said, but also *anti-capitalist*.

They were democratic societies, always.

They were cooperative societies, fraternal societies.

I make a systematic defense of the societies destroyed by imperialism.

They were the fact, they did not pretend to be the idea; despite their faults, they were neither to be hated nor condemned. They were content to be. In them, neither the word *failure* nor the word *avatar* had any meaning. They kept hope intact.

Whereas those are the only words that can, in all honesty, be applied to the European enterprises outside Europe. My only consolation is that periods of colonization pass, that nations sleep only for a time, and that peoples remain.

This being said, it seems that in certain circles they pretend to have discovered in me an "enemy of Europe" and a prophet of the return to the pre-European past.

For my part, I search in vain for the place where I could have expressed such views; where I ever underestimated the importance of Europe in the history of human thought; where I ever preached a *return* of any kind; where I ever claimed that there could be a *return*.

The truth is that I have said something very different: to wit, that the great historical tragedy of Africa has been not so much that it was too late in making contact with the rest of the world, as the manner in which that contact was brought about; that Europe began to "propagate" at a time when it had fallen into the hands of the most unscrupulous financiers and captains of industry; that it was our misfortune to encounter that particular Europe on our path, and that Europe is responsible before the human community for the highest heap of corpses in history.

In another connection, in judging colonization, I have added that Europe has gotten on very well indeed with all the local feudal lords who agreed to serve, woven a villainous complicity with them, rendered their tyranny more effective and more efficient, and that it has actually tended to prolong artificially the survival of local pasts in their most pernicious aspects.

I have said—and this is something very different—that colonialist Europe has grafted modern abuse onto ancient injustice, hateful racism onto old inequality.

That if I am attacked on the grounds of intent, I maintain that colonialist Europe is dishonest in trying to justify its colonizing activity *a posteriori* by the obvious material progress that has been achieved in certain fields under the colonial regime—since *sudden change* is always possible, in history as elsewhere; since no one knows at what stage of material development these same countries would have been if Europe had not intervened; since the introduction of technology into Africa and Asia, their administrative reorganization, in a word, their "Europeanization," was (as is proved by the example of Japan) in no way tied to the European *occupation;* since the

Europeanization of the non-European continents could have been accomplished otherwise than under the heel of Europe; since this movement of Europeanization was in progress; since it was even slowed down; since in any case it was distorted by the European takeover.

The proof is that at present it is the indigenous peoples of Africa and Asia who are demanding schools, and colonialist Europe which refuses them; that it is the African who is asking for ports and roads, and colonialist Europe which is niggardly on this score; that it is the colonized man who wants to move forward, and the colonizer who holds things back.

To go further, I make no secret of my opinion that at the present time the barbarism of Western Europe has reached an incredibly high level, being only surpassed—far surpassed, it is true—by the barbarism of the United States.

And I am not talking about Hitler, or the prison guard, or the adventurer, but about the "decent fellow" across the way; not about the member of the SS, or the gangster, but about the respectable bourgeois. In a time gone by, Léon Bloy innocently became indignant over the fact that swindlers, perjurers, forgers, thieves, and procurers were given the responsibility of "bringing to the Indies the example of Christian virtues."

We've made progress: today it is the possessor of the "Christian virtues" who intrigues—with no small success—for the honor of administering overseas territories according to the methods of forgers and torturers.

A sign that cruelty, mendacity, baseness, and corruption have sunk deep into the soul of the European bourgeoisie.

I repeat that I am not talking about Hitler, or the SS, or pogroms, or summary executions. But about a reaction caught unawares, a reflex permitted, a piece of cynicism tolerated. And if evidence is wanted, I could mention a scene of cannibalistic hysteria that I have been privileged to witness in the French National Assembly.

By Jove, my dear colleagues (as they say), I take off my hat to you (a cannibal's hat, of course).

Think of it! Ninety thousand dead in Madagascar! Indochina trampled underfoot, crushed to bits, assassinated, tortures brought back from the depths of the Middle Ages! And what a spectacle! The delicious shudder that roused the dozing deputies. The wild uproar! Bidault, looking like a communion wafer dipped in shit—unctuous and sanctimonious cannibalism; Moutet—the cannibalism of shady deals and sonorous nonsense; Coste-Floret—the cannibalism of an unlicked bear cub, a blundering fool.

Unforgettable, gentlemen! With fine phrases as cold and solemn as a mummy's wrappings they tie up the Madagascan. With a few conventional words they stab him for you. The time it takes to wet your whistle, they disembowel him for you. Fine work! Not a drop of blood will be wasted.

The ones who drink it straight, to the last drop. The ones like Ramadier, who smear their faces with it in the manner of Silenus;[3] Fontlup-Esperaber,[4] who starches his mustache with it, the walrus mustache of an ancient Gaul; old Desjardins bending over the emanations from the vat and intoxicating himself with them as with new wine. Violence! The violence of the weak. A significant thing: it is not the head of a civilization that begins to rot first. It is the heart.

I admit that as far as the health of Europe and civilization is concerned, these cries of "Kill! kill!" and "Let's see some blood," belched forth by trembling old men and virtuous young men educated by the Jesuit Fathers, make a much more disagreeable impression on me than the most sensational bank holdups that occur in Paris.

And that, mind you, is by no means an exception.

On the contrary, bourgeois swinishness is the rule. We've been on its trail for a century. We listen for it, we take it by surprise, we sniff it out, we follow it, lose it, find it again, shadow it, and every day it is more nauseatingly exposed. Oh! the racism of these gentlemen does not bother me. I do not become indignant over it. I merely examine it. I note it, and that is all. I am almost grateful to it for expressing itself openly and appearing in broad daylight, as a sign. A sign that the intrepid class which once stormed the Bastilles is now hamstrung. A sign that it feels itself to be mortal. A sign that it feels itself to be a corpse. And when the corpse starts to babble, you get this sort of thing:

> There was only too much truth in this first impulse of the Europeans who, *in the century of Columbus, refused to recognize as their fellow men the degraded inhabitants of the new world*. . . . One cannot gaze upon the savage for an instant without reading the anathema written, I do not say upon his soul alone, but *even on the external form of his body.*

And it's signed Joseph de Maistre.
(That's what is ground out by the mystical mill.)
And then you get this:

> From the selectionist point of view, I would look upon it as unfortunate if there should be a very great numerical expansion of

the yellow and black elements, which would be difficult to eliminate. However, if the society of the future is organized on a dualistic basis, *with a ruling class of dolichocephalic blonds and a class of inferior race confined to the roughest labor, it is possible that this latter role would fall to the yellow and black elements.* In this case, moreover, they would not be an inconvenience for the dolichocephalic blonds but an advantage. . . . *It must not be forgotten that* [slavery] *is no more abnormal than the domestication of the horse or the ox.* It is therefore possible that it may reappear in the future in one form or another. It is probably even inevitable that this will happen if the simplistic solution does not come about instead—that of a single superior race, leveled out by selection.

That's what is ground out by the scientific mill, and it's signed Lapouge.

And you also get this (from the literary mill this time):

I know that I must believe myself superior to the poor Bayas of the Mambéré. *I know that I must take pride in my blood.* When a superior man ceases to believe himself superior, he actually ceases to be superior. . . . *When a superior race ceases to believe itself a chosen race, it actually ceases to be a chosen race.*

And it's signed Psichari–soldier–of–Africa.

Translate it into newspaper jargon and you get Faguet:

The barbarian is of the same race, after all, as the Roman and the Greek. He is a cousin. The yellow man, the black man, is not our cousin at all. Here there is a real difference, a real distance, and a very great one: an *ethnological* distance. *After all, civilization has never yet been made except by whites.* . . . If Europe becomes yellow, there will certainly be a regression, a new period of darkness and confusion, that is, another Middle Ages.

And then lower, always lower, to the bottom of the pit, lower than the shovel can go, M. Jules Romains, of the Académie Française and the *Revue des Deux Mondes*. (It doesn't matter, of course, that M. Farigoule changes his name once again and here calls himself Salsette for the sake of convenience.)[5] The essential thing is that M. Jules Romains goes so far as to write this:

> I am willing to carry on a discussion only with people who agree to pose the following hypothesis: a France that had on its metropolitan soil ten million Blacks, five or six million of them in the valley of the Garonne. Would our valiant populations of the Southwest never have been touched by race prejudice? Would there not have been the slightest apprehension if the question had arisen of turning all powers over to these Negroes, the sons of slaves? . . . I once had opposite me a row of some twenty pure Blacks. . . . I will not even censure our Negroes and Negresses for chewing gum. I will only note . . . that this movement has the effect of emphasizing the jaws, and that the associations which come to mind evoke the equatorial forest rather than the procession of the Panathenaea . . . . The black race has not yet produced, will never produce, an Einstein, a Stravinsky, a Gershwin.

One idiotic comparison for another: since the prophet of the *Revue des Deux Mondes* and other places invites us to draw parallels between "widely separated" things, may I be permitted, Negro that I am, to think (no one being master of his free associations) that his voice has less in common with the rustling of the oak of Dodona—or even the vibrations of the cauldron—than with the braying of a Missouri ass.[6]

Once again, I systematically defend our old Negro civilizations: they were courteous civilizations.

So the real problem, you say, is to return to them. No, I repeat. We are not men for whom it is a question of "either-or." For us, the problem is not to make a utopian and sterile attempt to repeat the past, but to go beyond. It is not a dead society that we want to revive. We leave that to those who go in for exoticism. Nor is it the present colonial society that we wish to prolong, the most putrid carrion that ever rotted under the sun. It is a new society that we must create, with the help of all our brother slaves, a society rich with all the productive power of modern times, warm with all the fraternity of olden days.

For some examples showing that this is possible, we can look to the Soviet Union.

But let us return to M. Jules Romains:

One cannot say that the petty bourgeois has never read anything. On the contrary, he has read everything, devoured everything.

Only, his brain functions after the fashion of certain elementary types of digestive systems. It filters. And the filter lets through only what can nourish the thick skin of the bourgeois's clear conscience.

Before the arrival of the French in their country, the Vietnamese were people of an old culture, exquisite and refined. To recall this fact upsets the digestion of the Banque d'Indochine. Start the forgetting machine!

These Madagascans who are being tortured today, less than a century ago were poets, artists, administrators? Shhhhh! Keep your lips buttoned! And silence falls, silence as deep as a safe! Fortunately, there are still the Negroes. Ah! the Negroes! Let's talk about the Negroes!

All right, let's talk about them.

About the Sudanese empires? About the bronzes of Benin? Shango sculpture? That's all right with me; it will give us a change from all the sensationally bad art that adorns so many European capitals. About African music. Why not?

And about what the first explorers said, what they saw. . . . Not those who feed at the company mangers! But the d'Elbées, the Marchais, the Pigafettas! And then Frobenius! Say, you know who he was, Frobenius? And we read together: "Civilized to the marrow of their bones! The idea of the barbaric Negro is a European invention."

The petty bourgeois doesn't want to hear any more. With a twitch of his ears he flicks the idea away.

The idea, an annoying fly.

Therefore, comrade, you will hold as enemies—loftily, lucidly, consistently—not only sadistic governors and greedy bankers, not only prefects who torture and colonists who flog, not only corrupt, check-licking politicians and subservient judges, but likewise and for the same reason, venomous journalists, goitrous academics, wreathed in dollars and stupidity, ethnographers who go in for metaphysics, presumptuous Belgian theologians, chattering intellectuals born stinking out of the thigh of Nietzsche, the paternalists, the embracers, the corrupters, the back-slappers, the lovers of exoticism, the dividers, the agrarian sociologists, the hoodwinkers, the hoaxers, the hot-air artists, the humbugs, and in general, all those who, performing their functions in the sordid division of labor for the defense of Western bourgeois society, try in diverse ways and by infamous diversions to split up the forces of Progress—even if it means denying the very possibility of Progress—all of them tools of capitalism, all of them, openly or secretly, supporters of plundering colonialism, all of them responsible, all hateful, all slave-traders, all henceforth answerable for the violence of revolutionary action.

And sweep out all the obscurers, all the inventors of subterfuges, the charlatans and tricksters, the dealers in gobbledygook. And do not seek to know whether personally these gentlemen are in good or bad faith, whether personally they have good or bad intentions. Whether personally—that is, in the private conscience of Peter or Paul—they are or are not colonialists, because the essential thing is that their highly problematical subjective good faith is entirely irrelevant to the objective social implications of the evil work they perform as watchdogs of colonialism.

And in this connection, I cite as examples (purposely taken from very different disciplines):

—From Gourou, his book *Les Pays tropicaux,* in which, amid certain correct observations, there is expressed the fundamental thesis, biased and unacceptable, that there has never been a great tropical civilization, that great civilizations have existed only in temperate climates, that in every tropical country the germ of civilization comes, and can only come, from some other place outside the tropics, and that if the tropical countries are not under the biological curse of the racists, there at least hangs over them, with the same consequences, a no less effective geographical curse.

—From the Rev. Tempels, missionary and Belgian, his "Bantu philosophy," as slimy and fetid as one could wish, but discovered very opportunely, as Hinduism was discovered by others, in order to counteract the "communistic materialism" which, it seems, threatens to turn the Negroes into "moral vagabonds."

—From the historians or novelists of civilization (it's the same thing)—not from this one or that one, but from all of them, or almost all—their false objectivity, their chauvinism, their sly racism, their depraved passion for refusing to acknowledge any merit in the non-white races, especially the black-skinned races, their obsession with monopolizing all glory for their own race.

—From the psychologists, sociologists *et al.,* their views on "primitivism," their rigged investigations, their self-serving generalizations, their tendentious speculations, their insistence on the marginal, "separate" character of the non-whites, and—although each of these gentlemen, in order to impugn on higher authority the weakness of primitive thought, claims that his own is based on the firmest rationalism—their barbaric repudiation, for the sake of the cause, of Descartes's statement, the charter of universalism, that "reason . . . is found whole and entire in each man," and that "where individuals of the same species are concerned, there may be degrees in respect of their accidental qualities, but not in respect of their forms, or natures."[7]

But let us not go too quickly. It is worthwhile to follow a few of these gentlemen.

I shall not dwell upon the case of the historians, neither the historians of colonization nor the Egyptologists. The case of the former is too obvious, and as for the latter, the mechanism by which they delude their readers has been definitively taken apart by Sheikh Anta Diop in his book *Nations nègres et culture,* the most daring book yet written by a Negro and one which will without question play an important part in the awakening of Africa.[8]

Let us rather go back. To M. Gourou, to be exact.

Need I say that it is from a lofty height that the eminent scholar surveys the native populations, which "have taken no part" in the development of modern science? And that it is not from the effort of these populations, from their liberating struggle, from their concrete fight for life, freedom, and culture that he expects the salvation of the tropical countries to come, but from the good colonizer—since the law states categorically that "it is cultural elements developed in non-tropical regions which are ensuring and will ensure the progress of the tropical regions toward a larger population and a higher civilization."

I have said that M. Gourou's book contains some correct observations: "The tropical environment and the indigenous societies," he writes, drawing up the balance sheet on colonization, "have suffered from the introduction of techniques that are ill adapted to them, from corvées, porter service, forced labor, slavery, from the transplanting of workers from one region to another, sudden changes in the biological environment, and special new conditions that are less favorable."

A fine record! The look on the university rector's face! The look on the cabinet minister's face when he reads that! Our Gourou has slipped his leash; now we're in for it; he's going to tell everything; he's beginning: "The typical hot countries find themselves faced with the following dilemma: economic stagnation and protection of the natives or temporary economic development and regression of the natives." "Monsieur Gourou, this is very serious! I'm giving you a solemn warning: in this game it is your career which is at stake." So our Gourou chooses to back off and refrain from specifying that, if the dilemma exists, it exists only within the framework of the existing regime; that if this paradox constitutes an iron law, it is only the iron law of colonialist capitalism, therefore of a society that is not only perishable but already in the process of perishing.

What impure and worldly geography!

If there is anything better, it is the Rev. Tempels. Let them plunder and torture in the Congo, let the Belgian colonizer seize all the natural resources, let him stamp out all freedom, let him crush all pride—let him go in peace, the Reverend Father Tempels consents to all that. But take care! You are going to the Congo? Respect—I do not say native property (the great Belgian companies might take that as a dig at them), I do not say the freedom of the natives (the Belgian colonists might think that was subversive talk), I do not say the Congolese nation (the Belgian government might take it much amiss)—I say: You are going to the Congo? Respect the Bantu philosophy!

"It would be really outrageous," writes the Rev. Tempels, "if the white educator were to insist on destroying the black man's own, particular human spirit, which is the only reality that prevents us from considering him as an inferior being. It would be a crime against humanity, on the part of the colonizer, to emancipate the primitive races from that which is valid, from that which constitutes a kernel of truth in their traditional thought, etc."

What generosity, Father! And what zeal!

Now then, know that Bantu thought is essentially ontological; that Bantu ontology is based on the truly fundamental notions of a life force and a hierarchy of life forces; and that for the Bantu the ontological order which defines the world comes from God and, as a divine decree, must be respected.[9]

Wonderful! Everybody gains: the big companies, the colonists, the government—everybody except the Bantu, naturally.

Since Bantu thought is ontological, the Bantu only ask for satisfaction of an ontological nature. Decent wages! Comfortable housing! Food! These Bantu are pure spirits, I tell you: "What they desire first of all and above all is not the improvement of their economic or material situation, but the white man's recognition of and respect for their dignity as men, their full human value."

In short, you tip your hat to the Bantu life force, you give a wink to the immortal Bantu soul. And that's all it costs you! You have to admit you're getting off cheap!

As for the government, why should it complain? Since, the Rev. Tempels notes with obvious satisfaction, "from their first contact with the white men, the Bantu considered us from the only point of view that was possible to them, the point of view of their Bantu philosophy" and "*integrated us into their hierarchy of life forces at a very high level.*"

In other words, arrange it so that the white man, and particularly the Belgian, and even more particularly Albert or Leopold, takes his place at the head of the hierarchy of Bantu life forces, and you have done the trick. You will have brought this miracle to pass: *the Bantu god will take responsibility for the Belgian colonialist order, and any Bantu who dares to raise his hand against it will be guilty of sacrilege.*

As for M. Mannoni, in view of his book and his observations on the Madagascan soul, he deserves to be taken very seriously.

Follow him step by step through the ins and outs of his little conjuring tricks, and he will prove to you as clear as day that colonization is based on psychology, that there are in this world groups of men who, for unknown reasons, suffer from what must be called a dependency complex, that these groups are psychologically made for dependence; that they need dependence, that they crave it, ask for it, demand it; that this is the case with most of the colonized peoples and with the Madagascans in particular.

Away with racism! Away with colonialism! They smack too much of barbarism. M. Mannoni has something better: psychoanalysis. Embellished with existentialism, it gives astonishing results: the most down-at-the-heel clichés are re-soled for you and made good as new; the most absurd prejudices are explained and justified; and, as if by magic, the moon is turned into green cheese.

But listen to him:

> It is the destiny of the Occidental to face the obligation laid down by the commandment *Thou shalt leave thy father and thy mother.* This obligation is incomprehensible to the Madagascan. At a given time in his development, every European discovers in himself the desire . . . to break the bonds of dependency, to become the equal of his father. The Madagascan, never! He does not experience rivalry with the paternal authority, "manly protest," or Adlerian inferiority—ordeals through which the European must pass and which are like civilized forms . . . of the initiation rites by which one achieves manhood . . .

Don't let the subtleties of vocabulary, the new terminology, frighten you! You know the old refrain: "The-Negroes-are-big-children." They take it, they dress it up for you, tangle it up for you. The result is Mannoni. Once again, be reassured! At the start of the journey it may seem a bit difficult, but once you get there, you'll see, you will find all your baggage again. Nothing will be missing, not even the famous *white man's burden.* Therefore, give ear: "Through these ordeals" (reserved for the Occidental), "one triumphs over the infantile fear of abandonment and acquires freedom and autonomy, which are the most precious possessions and also the burdens of the Occidental."

And the Madagascan? you ask. A lying race of bondsmen, Kipling would say. M. Mannoni makes his diagnosis: "The Madagascan does not even try to imagine such a situation of abandonment. . . . He desires neither personal autonomy nor free responsibility." (Come on, you know how it is. These Negroes can't even imagine what freedom is. They don't want it, they don't demand it. It's the white agitators who put that into their heads. And if you gave it to them, they wouldn't know what to do with it.)

If you point out to M. Mannoni that the Madagascans have nevertheless revolted several times since the French occupation and again recently in 1947, M. Mannoni, faithful to his premises, will explain to you that that is purely neurotic behavior, a collective madness, a running amok; that, moreover, in this case it was not a question of the Madagascans' setting out to conquer real objectives but an "imaginary security," which obviously implies that the oppression of which they complain is an imaginary oppression. So clearly, so insanely imaginary, that one might even speak of monstrous ingratitude, according to the classic example of the Fijian who burns the drying-shed of the captain who has cured him of his wounds.

If you criticize the colonialism that drives the most peaceable populations to despair, M. Mannoni will explain to you that after all, the ones responsible *are not the colonialist whites* but the colonized Madagascans. Damn it all, they took the whites for gods and expected of them everything one expects of the divinity!

If you think the treatment applied to the Madagascan neurosis was a trifle rough, M. Mannoni, who has an answer for everything, will prove to you that the famous brutalities people talk about have been very greatly exaggerated, that it is all neurotic fabrication, that the tortures were imaginary tortures applied by "imaginary executioners." As for the French government, it showed itself singularly moderate, since it was content to arrest the Madagascan deputies, when it should have *sacrificed* them, if it had wanted to respect the laws of a healthy psychology.

I am not exaggerating. It is M. Mannoni speaking:

> Treading very classical paths, these Madagascans transformed their saints into martyrs, their saviors into scapegoats; they wanted to

wash their imaginary sins in the blood of their own gods. They were prepared, even at this price, or rather *only at this price,* to reverse their attitude once more. One feature of this dependent psychology would seem to be that, since no one can serve two masters, one of the two should be *sacrificed* to the other. The most agitated of the colonialists in Tananarive had a confused understanding of the essence of this psychology of sacrifice, and they demanded their victims. They besieged the High Commissioner's office, assuring him that if they were granted the blood of a few innocents, "everyone would be satisfied." This attitude, disgraceful from a human point of view, was *based on what was, on the whole, a fairly accurate perception of the emotional disturbances that the population of the high plateaux was going through.*

Obviously, it is only a step from this to absolving the bloodthirsty colonialists. M. Mannoni's "psychology" is as "disinterested," as "free," as M. Gourou's geography or the Rev. Tempels' missionary theology!

And the striking thing they all have in common is the persistent bourgeois attempt to reduce the most human problems to comfortable, hollow notions: the *idea* of the dependency complex in Mannoni, the ontological *idea* in the Rev. Tempels, the *idea* of "tropicality" in Gourou. What has become of the Banque d'Indochine in all that? And the Banque de Madagascar? And the bullwhip? And the taxes? And the handful of rice to the Madagascan or the *nhaqué*?[10] And the martyrs? And the innocent people murdered? And the blood-stained money piling up in your coffers, gentlemen? They have evaporated! Disappeared, intermingled, become unrecognizable in the realm of pale ratiocinations.

But there is one unfortunate thing for these gentlemen. It is that their bourgeois masters are less and less responsive to a tricky argument and are condemned increasingly to turn away from them and applaud others who are less subtle and more brutal. That is precisely what gives M. Yves Florenne a chance. And indeed, here, neatly arranged on the tray of the newspaper *Le Monde,* are his little offers of service. No possible surprises. Completely guaranteed, with proven efficacy, fully tested with conclusive results, here we have a form of racism, a French racism still not very sturdy, it is true, but promising. Listen to the man himself:

"Our reader" (a teacher who has had the audacity to contradict the irascible M. Florenne), ". . . contemplating two young half-breed girls, her pupils, has *a sense of pride at the feeling that there is a growing measure of integration with our French family.* . . . Would her response be the same if she saw, in reverse, France being integrated into the black family (or the yellow or red, it makes no difference), that is to say, becoming diluted, disappearing?"

It is clear that for M. Yves Florenne it is blood that makes France, and the foundations of the nation are biological: "Its people, its genius, are made of a thousand-year-old equilibrium that is at the same time vigorous and delicate, and . . . certain alarming disturbances of this equilibrium coincide with the massive and often dangerous infusion of foreign blood which it has had to undergo over the last thirty years."

In short, cross-breeding—that is the enemy. No more social crises! No more economic crises! All that is left are racial crises! Of course, humanism loses none of its prestige (we are in the Western world), but let us understand each other:

"It is not by losing itself in the human universe, with its blood and its spirit, that France will be universal, it is by remaining itself."
That is what the French bourgeoisie has come to, five years after the defeat of Hitler! And it is precisely in that that its historic punishment lies: to be condemned, returning to it as though driven by a vice, to chew over Hitler's vomit.

Because after all, M. Yves Florenne was still fussing over peasant novels, "dramas of the land," and stories of the evil eye when, with a far more evil eye than the rustic hero of some tale of witchcraft, Hitler was announcing: "The supreme goal of the People-State is to preserve the original elements of the race which, by spreading culture, create the beauty and dignity of a superior humanity."

M. Yves Florenne is aware of this direct descent.

And he is far from being embarrassed by it.

Fine. That's his right.

As it is not our right to be indignant about it.

Because, after all, we must resign ourselves to the inevitable and say to ourselves, once and for all, that the bourgeoisie is condemned to become every day more snarling, more openly ferocious, more shameless, more summarily barbarous; that it is an implacable law that every decadent class finds itself turned into a receptacle into which there flow all the dirty waters of history; that it is a universal law that before it disappears, every class must first disgrace itself completely, on all fronts, and that it is with their heads buried in the dunghill that dying societies utter their swan songs.

The dossier is indeed overwhelming.

A beast that by the elementary exercise of its vitality spills blood and sows death—you remember that historically it was in the form of this fierce archetype that capitalist society first revealed itself to the best minds and consciences.

Since then the animal has become anemic, it is losing its hair, its hide is no longer glossy, but the ferocity has remained, barely mixed with sadism. It is easy to blame it on Hitler. On Rosenberg. On Jünger and the others. On the SS.

But what about this: "Everything in this world reeks of crime: the newspaper, the wall, the countenance of man."

Baudelaire said that, before Hitler was born!

Which proves that the evil has a deeper source.

And Isidore Ducasse, Comte de Lautréamont![11]

In this connection, it is high time to dissipate the atmosphere of scandal that has been created around the *Chants de Maldoror.* Monstrosity? Literary meteorite? Delirium of a sick imagination? Come, now! How convenient it is!

The truth is that Lautréamont had only to look the iron man forged by capitalist society squarely in the eye to perceive the *monster,* the everyday monster, his hero.

No one denies the veracity of Balzac.

But wait a moment: take Vautrin, let him be just back from the tropics, give him the wings of the archangel and the shivers of malaria, let him be accompanied through the streets of Paris by an escort of Uruguayan vampires and carnivorous ants, and you will have Maldoror.[12]

The setting is changed, but it is the same world, the same man, hard, inflexible, unscrupulous, fond, if ever a man was, of "the flesh of other men."

To digress for a moment within my digression, I believe that the day will come when, with all the elements gathered together, all the sources analyzed, all the circumstances of the work elucidated, it will be possible to give the *Chants de Maldoror* a materialistic and historical interpretation which will bring to light an altogether unrecognized aspect of this frenzied epic, its implacable denunciation of a very particular form of society, as it could not escape the sharpest eyes around the year 1865.

Before that, of course, we will have had to clear away the occultist and metaphysical commentaries that obscure the path; to re-establish the importance of certain neglected stanzas—for example, that strangest passage of all, the one concerning the mine of lice, in which we will consent to see nothing more or less than the denunciation of the evil power of gold and the hoarding up of money; to restore to its true place the admirable episode of the omnibus, and be willing to find in it very simply what is there, to wit, the scarcely allegorical picture of a society in which the privileged, comfortably seated, refuse to move closer together so as to make room for the new arrival. And—be it said in passing—who welcomes the child who has been callously rejected? The people! Represented here by the ragpicker. Baudelaire's ragpicker:

> Paying no heed to the spies of the cops, his thralls,
> He pours his heart out in stupendous schemes.
> He takes great oaths and dictates sublime laws,
> Casts down the wicked, aids the victims' cause.[13]

Then it will be understood, will it not, that the enemy whom Lautréamont has made *the enemy,* the cannibalistic, brain-devouring "Creator," the sadist perched on "a throne made of human excrement and gold," the hypocrite, the debauchee, the idler who "eats the bread of others" and who from time to time is found dead drunk, "drunk as a bedbug that has swallowed three barrels of blood during the night," it will be understood that it is not beyond the clouds that one must look for that creator, but that we are more likely to find him in Desfossés's business directory and on some comfortable executive board!

But let that be.

The moralists can do nothing about it.

Whether one likes it or not, the bourgeoisie, as a class, is condemned to take responsibility for all the barbarism of history, the tortures of the Middle Ages and the Inquisition, warmongering and the appeal to the *raison d'Etat,* racism and slavery, in short everything against which it protested in unforgettable terms at the time when, as the attacking class, it was the incarnation of human progress.

The moralists can do nothing about it. There is a law of *progressive dehumanization* in accordance with which henceforth on the agenda of the bourgeoisie there is—there can be—nothing but violence, corruption, and barbarism.

I almost forgot hatred, lying, conceit.

I almost forgot M. Roger Caillois.[14]

Well then: M. Caillois, who from time immemorial has been given the mission to teach a lax and slipshod age rigorous thought and dignified style, M. Caillois, therefore, has just been moved to mighty wrath. Why?

Because of the great betrayal of Western ethnography which, with a deplorable deterioration of its sense of responsibility, has been using all its ingenuity of late to cast doubt upon the overall superiority of Western civilization over the exotic civilizations.

Now at last M. Caillois takes the field.

Europe has this capacity for raising up heroic saviors at the most critical moments.

It is unpardonable on our part not to remember M. Massis, who, around 1927, embarked on a crusade for the defense of the West.

We want to make sure that a better fate is in store for M. Caillois, who, in order to defend the same sacred cause, transforms his pen into a good Toledo dagger.

What did M. Massis say? He deplored the fact that "the destiny of Western civilization, and indeed the destiny of man," were now threatened; that an attempt was being made on all sides "to appeal to our anxieties, to challenge the claims made for our culture, to call into question the most essential part of what we possess," and he swore to make war upon these "disastrous prophets."

M. Caillois identifies the enemy no differently. It is those "European intellectuals" who for the last fifty years, "because of

exceptionally sharp disappointment and bitterness," have relent-
lessly "repudiated the various ideals of their culture," and who by
so doing maintain, "especially in Europe, a tenacious malaise."

It is this malaise, this anxiety, which M. Caillois, for his part,
means to put to an end.[15]

And indeed, no personage since the Englishman of the Victorian
age has ever surveyed history with a conscience more serene and less
clouded with doubt.

His doctrine? It has the virtue of simplicity.

That the West invented science. That the West alone knows how
to think; that at the borders of the Western world there begins the
shadowy realm of primitive thinking, which, dominated by the notion
of participation, incapable of logic, is the very model of faulty thinking.

At this point one gives a start. One reminds M. Caillois that the
famous law of participation invented by Lévy-Bruhl was repudiated
by Lévy-Bruhl himself; that in the evening of his life he proclaimed
to the world that he had been wrong in "trying to define a characteristic, that was peculiar to the primitive mentality so far as logic
was concerned"; that, on the contrary, he had become convinced
that "these minds do not differ from ours at all from the point of
view of logic. . . . Therefore, [that they] cannot tolerate a formal
contradiction any more than we can. . . . Therefore, [that they] reject
as we do, by a kind of mental reflex, that which is logically
impossible."[16]

A waste of time! M. Caillois considers the rectification to be null
and void. For M. Caillois, the true Lévy-Bruhl can only be the
Lévy-Bruhl who says that primitive man talks raving nonsense.

Of course, there remain a few small facts that resist this doctrine.
To wit, the invention of arithmetic and geometry by the Egyptians.
To wit, the discovery of astronomy by the Assyrians. To wit, the

birth of chemistry among the Arabs. To wit, the appearance of rationalism in Islam at a time when Western thought had a furiously pre-logical cast to it. But M. Caillois soon puts these impertinent details in their place, since it is a strict principle that "a discovery which does not fit into a whole" is, precisely, only a detail, that is to say, a negligible nothing.

As you can imagine, once off to such a good start, M. Caillois doesn't stop half way.

Having annexed science, he's going to claim ethics too.

Just think of it! M. Caillois has never eaten anyone! M. Caillois has never dreamed of finishing off an invalid! It has never occurred to M. Caillois to shorten the days of his aged parents! Well, there you have it, the superiority of the West: "That discipline of life which tries to ensure that the human person is sufficiently respected so that it is not considered normal to eliminate the old and the infirm."

The conclusion is inescapable: compared to the cannibals, the dismemberers, and other lesser breeds, Europe and the West are the incarnation of respect for human dignity.

But let us move on, and quickly, lest our thoughts wander to Algiers, Morocco, and other places where, as I write these very words, so many valiant sons of the West, in the semi-darkness of dungeons, are lavishing upon their inferior African brothers, with such tireless attention, those authentic marks of respect for human dignity which are called, in technical terms, "electricity," "the bathtub," and "the bottleneck."

Let us press on: M. Caillois has not yet reached the end of his list of outstanding achievements. After scientific superiority and moral superiority comes religious superiority.

Here, M. Caillois is careful not to let himself be deceived by the empty prestige of the Orient. Asia, mother of gods, perhaps. Anyway,

Europe, mistress of rites. And see how wonderful it is: on the one hand—outside of Europe—ceremonies of the voodoo type, with all their "ludicrous masquerade, their collective frenzy, their wild alcoholism, their crude exploitation of a naïve fervor," and on the other hand—in Europe—those authentic values which Chateaubriand was already celebrating in his *Génie du christianisme:* "The dogmas and mysteries of the Catholic religion, its liturgy, the symbolism of its sculptors and the glory of the plainsong."

Lastly, a final cause for satisfaction:

Gobineau said: "The only history is white." M. Caillois, in turn, observes: "The only ethnography is white." It is the West that studies the ethnography of the others, not the others who study the ethnography of the West.

A cause for the greatest jubilation, is it not?

And the museums of which M. Caillois is so proud, not for one minute does it cross his mind that, all things considered, it would have been better not to have needed them; that Europe would have done better to tolerate the non-European civilizations at its side, leaving them alive, dynamic and prosperous, whole and not mutilated; that it would have been better to let them develop and fulfill themselves than to present for our admiration, duly labelled, their dead and scattered parts; that anyway, the museum by itself is nothing; that it means nothing, that it can say nothing, when smug self-satisfaction rots the eyes, when a secret contempt for others withers the heart, when racism, admitted or not, dries up sympathy; that it means nothing if its only purpose is to feed the delights of vanity; that after all, the honest contemporary of Saint Louis, who fought Islam but respected it, had a better chance of *knowing* it than do our contemporaries (even if they have a smattering of ethnographic literature), who despise it.

No, in the scales of knowledge all the museums in the world will never weigh so much as one spark of human sympathy.

And what is the conclusion of all that?

Let us be fair; M. Caillois is moderate.

Having established the superiority of the West in all fields, and having thus re-established a wholesome and extremely valuable hierarchy, M. Caillois gives immediate proof of this superiority by concluding that no one should be exterminated. With him the Negroes are sure that they will not be lynched; the Jews, that they will not feed new bonfires. There is just one thing: it is important for it to be clearly understood that the Negroes, Jews, and Australians owe this tolerance not to their respective merits, but to the magnanimity of M. Caillois; not to the dictates of science, which can offer only ephemeral truths, but to a decree of M. Caillois's conscience, which can only be absolute; that this tolerance has no conditions, no guarantees, unless it be M. Caillois's sense of his duty to himself.

Perhaps science will one day declare that the backward cultures and retarded peoples which constitute so many dead weights and impedimenta on humanity's path must be cleared away, but we are assured that at the critical moment the conscience of M. Caillois, transformed on the spot from a clear conscience into a noble conscience, will arrest the executioner's arm and pronounce the *salvus sis*.

To which we are indebted for the following juicy note:

> For me, the question of the equality of races, peoples, or cultures has meaning only if we are talking about an equality in law, not an equality in fact. In the same way, men who are blind, maimed, sick, feeble-minded, ignorant, or poor (one could hardly be nicer to the non-Occidentals) are not respectively equal, in the material sense of

the word, to those who are strong, clear-sighted, whole, healthy, intelligent, cultured, or rich. The latter have greater capacities which, by the way, do not give them more rights but only more duties. . . . Similarly, whether for biological or historical reasons, there exist at present differences in level, power, and value among the various cultures. These differences entail an inequality in fact. They in no way justify an inequality of rights in favor of the so-called superior peoples, as racism would have it. Rather, they confer upon them additional tasks and an increased responsibility.

Additional tasks? What are they, if not the tasks of ruling the world?

Increased responsibility? What is it, if not responsibility for the world?

And Caillois-Atlas charitably plants his feet firmly in the dust and once again raises to his sturdy shoulders the inevitable white man's burden.

The reader must excuse me for having talked about M. Caillois at such length. It is not that I overestimate to any degree whatever the intrinsic value of his "philosophy"—the reader will have been able to judge how seriously one should take a thinker who, while claiming to be dedicated to rigorous logic, sacrifices so willingly to prejudice and wallows so voluptuously in clichés. But his views are worth special attention because they are significant.

Significant of what?

Of the state of mind of thousands upon thousands of Europeans or, to be very precise, of the state of mind of the Western petty bourgeoisie.

Significant of what?

Of this: that at the very time when it most often mouths the word, the West has never been further from being able to live a true humanism—a humanism made to the measure of the world.

One of the values invented by the bourgeoisie in former times and launched throughout the world was *man*—and we have seen what has become of that. The other was the nation.

It is a fact: the *nation* is a bourgeois phenomenon.

Exactly; but if I turn my attention from *man* to *nations,* I note that here too there is great danger; that colonial enterprise is to the modern world what Roman imperialism was to the ancient world: the prelude to Disaster and the forerunner of Catastrophe. Come, now! The Indians massacred, the Moslem world drained of itself, the Chinese world defiled and perverted for a good century; the Negro world disqualified; mighty voices stilled forever; homes scattered to the wind; all this wreckage, all this waste, humanity reduced to a monologue, and you think all that does not have its price? The truth is that this policy *cannot but bring about the ruin of*

Europe itself, and that Europe, if it is not careful, will perish from the void it has created around itself.

They thought they were only slaughtering Indians, or Hindus, or South Sea Islanders, or Africans. They have in fact overthrown, one after another, the ramparts behind which European civilization could have developed freely.

I know how fallacious historical parallels are, particularly the one I am about to draw. Nevertheless, permit me to quote a page from Edgar Quinet for the not inconsiderable element of truth which it contains and which is worth pondering.

Here it is:

> People ask why barbarism emerged all at once in ancient civilization. I believe I know the answer. It is surprising that so simple a cause is not obvious to everyone. The system of ancient civilization was composed of a certain number of nationalities, of countries which, although they seemed to be enemies, or were even ignorant of each other, protected, supported, and guarded one another. When the expanding Roman Empire undertook to conquer and destroy these groups of nations, the dazzled sophists thought they saw at the end of this road humanity triumphant in Rome. They talked about the unity of the human spirit; it was only a dream. It happened that these nationalities were so many bulwarks protecting Rome itself. . . . Thus when Rome, in its alleged triumphal march toward a single civilization, had destroyed, one after the other, Carthage, Egypt, Greece, Judea, Persia, Dacia, and Cisalpine and Transalpine Gaul, it came to pass that it had itself swallowed up the dikes that protected it against the human ocean under which it was to perish. The magnanimous Caesar, by crushing the two Gauls, only paved the way for the Teutons. So many societies, so many languages extinguished, so many cities, rights, homes annihilated, created a void around Rome, and in those places which were not invaded by the barbarians, barbarism was born spontaneously. The vanquished Gauls changed into Bagaudes. Thus the violent downfall, the progressive extirpation of

individual cities, caused the crumbling of ancient civilization. That social edifice was supported by the various nationalities as by so many different columns of marble or porphyry.

When, to the applause of the wise men of the time, each of these living columns had been demolished, the edifice came crashing down; and the wise men of our day are still trying to understand how such mighty ruins could have been made in a moment's time.

And now I ask: what else has bourgeois Europe done? It has undermined civilizations, destroyed countries, ruined nationalities, extirpated "the root of diversity." No more dikes, no more bulwarks. The hour of the barbarian is at hand. The modern barbarian. The American hour. Violence, excess, waste, mercantilism, bluff, conformism, stupidity, vulgarity, disorder.

In 1913, Ambassador Page wrote to Wilson:

"The future of the world belongs to us. . . . Now what are we going to do with the leadership of the world presently when it clearly falls into our hands?"

And in 1914: "What are we going to do with this England and this Empire, presently, when economic forces unmistakably put the leadership of the race in our hands?"

This Empire . . . And the others . . .

And indeed, do you not see how ostentatiously these gentlemen have just unfurled the banner of anti-colonialism?

"Aid to the disinherited countries," says Truman. "The time of the old colonialism has passed." That's also Truman.

Which means that American high finance considers that the time has come to raid every colony in the world. So, dear friends, here you have to be careful!

I know that some of you, disgusted with Europe, with all that hideous mess which you did not witness by choice, are turning—oh!

in no great numbers—toward America and getting used to looking upon that country as a possible liberator.

"What a godsend!" you think.

"The bulldozers! The massive investments of capital! The roads! The ports!"

"But American racism!"

"So what? European racism in the colonies has inured us to it!"

And there we are, ready to run the great Yankee risk.

So, once again, be careful!

American domination—the only domination from which one never recovers. I mean from which one never recovers unscarred.

And since you are talking about factories and industries, do you not see the tremendous factory hysterically spitting out its cinders in the heart of our forests or deep in the bush, the factory for the production of lackeys; do you not see the prodigious mechanization, the mechanization of man; the gigantic rape of everything intimate, undamaged, undefiled that, despoiled as we are, our human spirit has still managed to preserve; the machine, yes, have you never seen it, the machine for crushing, for grinding, for degrading peoples?

So that the danger is immense.

So that unless, in Africa, in the South Sea Islands, in Madagascar (that is, at the gates of South Africa), in the West Indies (that is, at the gates of America), Western Europe undertakes on its own initiative a policy of *nationalities*, a new policy founded on respect for peoples and cultures—nay, more—unless Europe galvanizes the dying cultures or raises up new ones, unless it becomes the awakener of countries and civilizations (this being said without taking into account the admirable resistance of the colonial peoples primarily symbolized at present by Vietnam, but also by the Africa of the Rassemblement Démocratique Africain), Europe will have deprived itself of its last *chance* and, with its own hands, drawn up over itself the pall of mortal darkness.

Which comes down to saying that the salvation of Europe is not a matter of a revolution in methods. It is a matter of the Revolution—the one which, until such time as there is a classless society, will substitute for the narrow tyranny of a dehumanized bourgeoisie the preponderance of the only class that still has a universal mission, because it suffers in its flesh from all the wrongs of history, from all the universal wrongs: the proletariat.

AN INTERVIEW WITH AIMÉ CÉSAIRE

Conducted by René Depestre

The following interview with Aimé Césaire was conducted by Haitian poet and militant René Depestre at the Cultural Congress of Havana in 1967. It first appeared in Poesias, *an anthology of Césaire's writings published by Casa de las Américas. It has been translated from the Spanish by Maro Riofrancos.*

RENÉ DEPESTRE: The critic Lilyan Kesteloot has written that *Return to My Native Land* is an autobiographical book. Is this opinion well founded?

AIMÉ CÉSAIRE: Certainly. It is an autobiographical book, but at the same time it is a book in which I tried to gain an understanding of myself. In a certain sense it is closer to the truth than a biography. You must remember that it is a young person's book: I wrote it just after I had finished my studies and had come back to Martinique. These were my first contacts with my country after an absence of ten years, so I really found myself assaulted by a sea of impressions and images. At the same time I felt a deep anguish over the prospects for Martinique.

R.D.: How old were you when you wrote the book?

A.C.: I must have been around twenty-six.

R.D.: Nevertheless, what is striking about it is its great maturity.

A.C.: It was my first published work, but actually it contains poems that I had accumulated, or done progressively. I remember having written quite a few poems before these.

R.D.: But they have never been published.

A.C.: They haven't been published because I wasn't very happy with them. The friends to whom I showed them found them interesting, but they didn't satisfy me.

R.D.: Why?

A.C.: Because I don't think I had found a form that was my own. I was still under the influence of the French poets. In short, if *Return to My Native Land* took the form of a prose poem, it was truly by chance. Even though I wanted to break with French literary traditions, I did not actually free myself from them until the moment I decided to turn my back on poetry. In fact, you could say that I became a poet by renouncing poetry. Do you see what I mean? Poetry was for me the only way to break the stranglehold the accepted French form held on me.

R.D.: In her introduction to your selected poems published by Editions Seghers, Lilyan Kesteloot names Mallarmé, Claudel, Rimbaud, and Lautréamont among the poets who have influenced you.

A.C.: Lautréamont and Rimbaud were a great revelation for many poets of my generation. I must also say that I don't renounce Claudel. His poetry, in *Tête d'Or* for example, made a deep impression on me.

R.D.: There is no doubt that it is great poetry.

A.C.: Yes, truly great poetry, very beautiful. Naturally, there were many things about Claudel that irritated me, but I have always considered him a great craftsman with language.

R.D.: Your *Return to My Native Land* bears the stamp of personal experience, your experience as a Martinican youth, and it also deals with the itineraries of the Negro race in the Antilles, where French influences are not decisive.

A.C.: I don't deny French influences myself. Whether I want to or not, as a poet I express myself in French, and clearly French literature has influenced me. But I want to emphasize very strongly that—while using as a point of departure the elements that French literature gave me—at the same time I have always striven to create a new language, one capable of communicating the African heritage. In other words, for me French was a tool that I wanted to use in developing a new means of expression. I wanted to create an Antillean French, a black French that, while still being French, had a black character.

R.D.: Has surrealism been instrumental in your effort to discover this new French language?

A.C.: I was ready to accept surrealism because I already had advanced on my own, using as my starting points the same authors that had influenced the surrealist poets. Their thinking and mine had common reference points. Surrealism provided me with what I had been confusedly searching for. I have accepted it joyfully because in it I have found more of a confirmation than a revelation. It was a weapon that exploded the French language. It shook up absolutely everything. This was very important because the traditional forms—burdensome, overused forms—were crushing me.

R.D.: This was what interested you in the surrealist movement . . .

A.C.: Surrealism interested me to the extent that it was a liberating factor.

R.D.: So you were very sensitive to the concept of liberation that surrealism contained. Surrealism called forth deep and unconscious forces.

A.C.: Exactly. And my thinking followed these lines: Well then, if I apply the surrealist approach to my particular situation, I can summon up these unconscious forces. This, for me, was a call to Africa. I said to myself: it's true that superficially we are French, we bear the marks of French customs; we have been branded by Cartesian philosophy, by French rhetoric; but if we break with all that, if we plumb the depths, then what we will find is fundamentally black.

R.D.: In other words, it was a process of disalienation.

A.C.: Yes, a process of disalienation, that's how I interpreted surrealism.

R.D.: That's how surrealism has manifested itself in your work: as an effort to reclaim your authentic character, and in a way as an effort to reclaim the African heritage.

A.C.: Absolutely.

R.D.: And as a process of detoxification.

A.C.: A plunge into the depths. It was a plunge into Africa for me.

R.D.: It was a way of emancipating your consciousness.

A.C.: Yes, I felt that beneath the social being would be found a profound being, over whom all sorts of ancestral layers and alluviums had been deposited.

R.D.: Now, I would like to go back to the period in your life in Paris when you collaborated with Léopold Sédar Senghor and Léon-Gontran Damas on the small periodical *L'Etudiant noir*. Was this the first stage of the Negritude expressed in *Return to My Native Land*?

A.C.: Yes, it was already Negritude, as we conceived of it then. There were two tendencies within our group. On the one hand, there were people from the left, Communists at that time, such as J. Monnerot, E. Léro, and René Ménil. They were Communists, and therefore we supported them. But very soon I had to reproach them—and perhaps I owe this to Senghor—for being French Communists. There was nothing to distinguish them either from the French surrealists or from the French Communists. In other words, their poems were colorless.

R.D.: They were not attempting disalienation.

A.C.: In my opinion they bore the marks of assimilation. At that time Martinican students assimilated either with the French rightists or with the French leftists. But it was always a process of assimilation.

R.D.: At bottom what separated you from the Communist Martinican students at that time was the Negro question.

A.C.: Yes, the Negro question. At that time I criticized the Communists for forgetting our Negro characteristics. They acted like Communists, which was all right, but they acted like abstract Communists. I maintained that the political question could not do away with our condition as Negroes. We are Negroes, with a great number of historical peculiarities. I suppose that I must have been influenced by Senghor in this. At the time I knew absolutely nothing about Africa. Soon afterward I met Senghor, and he told me a great deal about Africa. He made an enormous impression on me: I am indebted to him for the revelation of Africa and African singularity. And I tried to develop a theory to encompass all of my reality.

R.D.: You have tried to particularize Communism . . .

A.C.: Yes, it is a very old tendency of mine. Even then Communists would reproach me for speaking of the Negro problem—they called it my racism. But I would answer: Marx is all right, but we need to complete Marx. I felt that the emancipation of the Negro consisted of more than just a political emancipation.

R.D.: Do you see a relationship among the movements between the two world wars connected to *L'Etudiant noir,* the Negro Renaissance Movement in the United States, *La Revue indigène* in Haiti, and *Negrismo* in Cuba?

A.C.: I was not influenced by those other movements because I did not know of them. But I'm sure they are parallel movements.

R.D.: How do you explain the emergence, in the years between the two world wars, of these parallel movements—in Haiti, the United States, Cuba, Brazil, Martinique, etc.—that recognized the cultural particularities of Africa?

A.C.: I believe that at that time in the history of the world there was a coming to consciousness among Negroes, and this manifested itself in movements that had no relationship to each other.

R.D.: There was the extraordinary phenomenon of jazz.

A.C.: Yes, there was the phenomenon of jazz. There was the Marcus Garvey movement. I remember very well that even when I was a child I had heard people speak of Garvey.

R.D.: Marcus Garvey was a sort of Negro prophet whose speeches had galvanized the Negro masses of the United States. His objective was to take all the American Negroes to Africa.

A.C.: He inspired a mass movement, and for several years he was a symbol to American Negroes. In France there was a newspaper called *Le Cri des nègres.*

R.D.: I believe that Haitians like Dr. Sajous, Jacques Roumain, and Jean Price-Mars collaborated on that newspaper. There were also six issues of *La Revue du monde noir,* written by René Maran, Claude McKay, Price-Mars, the Achille brothers, Sajous, and others.

A.C.: I remember very well that around that time we read the poems of Langston Hughes and Claude McKay. I knew very well who McKay was because in 1929 or 1930 an anthology of American Negro poetry appeared in Paris. And McKay's novel, *Banjo*—describing the life of dock workers in Marseilles—was published in 1930. This was really one of the first works in which an author spoke of the Negro and gave him a certain literary dignity. I must say, therefore, that although I was not directly influenced by any American Negroes, at least I felt that the movement in the United States created an atmosphere that was indispensable for a very clear coming to consciousness. During the 1920s and 1930s I came under three main influences, roughly speaking. The first was the French literary influence, through the works of Mallarmé, Rimbaud, Lautréamont and Claudel. The second was Africa. I knew very little about Africa, but I deepened my knowledge through ethnographic studies.

R.D.: I believe that European ethnographers have made a contribution to the development of the concept of Negritude.

A.C.: Certainly. And as for the third influence, it was the Negro Renaissance Movement in the United States, which did not influence me directly but still created an atmosphere which allowed me to become conscious of the solidarity of the black world.

R.D.: At that time you were not aware, for example, of developments along the same lines in Haiti, centered around *La Revue indigène* and Jean Price-Mars's book, *Ainsi parla l'oncle.*

A.C.: No, it was only later that I discovered the Haitian movement and Price-Mars's famous book.

R.D.: How would you describe your encounter with Senghor, the encounter between Antillean Negritude and African Negritude? Was it the result of a particular event or of a parallel development of consciousness?

A.C.: It was simply that in Paris at that time there were a few dozen Negroes of diverse origins. There were Africans, like Senghor, Guianans, Haitians, North Americans, Antilleans, etc. This was very important for me.

R.D.: In this circle of Negroes in Paris, was there a consciousness of the importance of African culture?

A.C.: Yes, as well as an awareness of the solidarity among blacks. We had come from different parts of the world. It was our first meeting. We were discovering ourselves. This was very important.

R.D.: It was extraordinarily important. How did you come to develop the concept of Negritude?

A.C.: I have a feeling that it was somewhat of a collective creation. I used the term first, that's true. But it's possible we talked about it in our group. It was really a resistance to the politics of assimilation. Until that time, until my generation, the French and the English—but especially the French—had followed the politics of assimilation unrestrainedly. We didn't know what Africa was. Europeans despised everything about Africa, and in France people spoke of a civilized world and a barbarian world. The barbarian world was Africa, and the civilized world was Europe. Therefore the best thing one could do with an African was to assimilate him: the ideal was to turn him into a Frenchman with black skin.

R.D.: Haiti experienced a similar phenomenon at the beginning of the nineteenth century. There is an entire Haitian pseudo-literature, created by authors who allowed themselves to be assimilated. The independence of Haiti, our first independence, was a violent attack against the French presence in our country, but our first authors did not attack French cultural values with equal force. They did not proceed toward a decolonization of their consciousness.

A.C.: This is what is known as *bovarisme*. In Martinique also we were in the midst of *bovarisme*. I still remember a poor little Martinican pharmacist who passed the time writing poems and sonnets which he sent to literary contests, such as the Floral Games of Toulouse. He felt very proud when one of his poems won a prize. One day he told me that the judges hadn't even realized that his poems were written by a man of color. To put it in other words, his poetry was so impersonal that it made him proud. He was filled with pride by something I would have considered a crushing condemnation.

R.D.: It was a case of total alienation.

A.C.: I think you've put your finger on it. Our struggle was a struggle against alienation. That struggle gave birth to Negritude. Because Antilleans were ashamed of being Negroes, they searched for all sorts of euphemisms for Negro: they would say a man of color, a dark-complexioned man, and other idiocies like that.

R.D.: Yes, real idiocies.

A.C.: That's when we adopted the word *nègre,* as a term of defiance. It was a defiant name. To some extent it was a reaction of enraged youth. Since there was shame about the word *nègre,* we chose the word *nègre.* I must say that when we founded *L'Etudiant noir,* I really wanted to call it *L'Etudiant nègre,* but there was a great resistance to that among the Antilleans.

R.D.: Some thought that the word *nègre* was offensive.

A.C.: Yes, too offensive, too aggressive, and then I took the liberty of speaking of *négritude.* There was in us a defiant will, and we found a violent affirmation in the words *nègre,* and *négritude.*

R.D.: In *Return to My Native Land* you have stated that Haiti was the cradle of Negritude. In your words, "Haiti, where Negritude stood on its feet for the first time." Then, in your opinion, the history of our country is in a certain sense the prehistory of Negritude. How have you applied the concept of Negritude to the history of Haiti?

A.C.: Well, after my discovery of the North American Negro and my discovery of Africa, I went on to explore the totality of the black world, and that is how I came upon the history of Haiti. I love Martinique, but it is an alienated land, while Haiti represented for me the heroic Antilles, the African Antilles. I began to make connections between the Antilles and Africa, and Haiti is the most African of the Antilles. It is at the same time a country with a marvelous history: the first Negro epic of the New World was written by Haitians, people like Toussaint L'Ouverture, Henri Christophe, Jean-Jacques Dessalines, etc. Haiti is not very well known in Martinique. I am one of the few Martinicans who know and love Haiti.

R.D.: Then for you the first independence struggle in Haiti was a confirmation, a demonstration of the concept of Negritude. Our national history is Negritude in action.

A.C.: Yes, Negritude in action. Haiti is the country where Negro people stood up for the first time, affirming their determination to shape a new world, a free world.

R.D.: During all of the nineteenth century there were men in Haiti who, without using the term Negritude, understood the signifi- cance of Haiti for world history. Haitian authors, such as Han- nibal Price and Louis-Joseph Janvier, were already speaking of the need to reclaim black cultural and aesthetic values. A genius like Anténor Firmin wrote in Paris a book entitled *De l'égalité des races humaines,* in which he tried to re-evaluate African culture in Haiti in order to combat the total and colorless assimilation that was characteristic of our early authors. You could say that beginning with the second half of the nineteenth century, some Haitian authors—Justin Lhérisson, Frédéric Marcelin, Fernand Hibbert, and Antoine Innocent—began to discover the peculiarities of our country, the fact that we had an African past, that the slave was not born yesterday, that voodoo was an important element in the development of our national culture. Now it is necessary to examine the concept of Negritude more closely. Negritude has lived through all kinds of adventures. I don't believe that this concept is always understood in its original sense, with its explosive nature. In fact, there are people today in Paris and other places whose objectives are very different from those of *Return to My Native Land.*

A.C.: I would like to say that everyone has his own Negritude. There has been too much theorizing about Negritude. I have tried not to overdo it, out of a sense of modesty. But if someone asks me what my conception of Negritude is, I answer that above all it is a concrete rather than an abstract coming to consciousness. What I have been telling you about—the atmosphere in which we lived, an atmosphere of assimilation in which Negro people were ashamed of themselves—has great importance. We lived in an atmosphere of rejection, and we developed an inferiority complex. I have always thought that the black man was searching for his identity. And it has seemed to me that if what we want is to establish this identity, then we must have a concrete consciousness of what we are—that is, of the first fact of our lives: that we are black; that we were black and have a history, a history that contains certain cultural elements of great value; and that Negroes were not, as you put it, born yesterday, because there have been beautiful and important black civilizations. At the time we began to write, people could write a history of world civilization without devoting a single chapter to Africa, as if Africa had made no contributions to the world. Therefore we affirmed that we were Negroes and that we were proud of it, and that we thought that Africa was not some sort of blank page in the history of humanity; in sum, we asserted that our Negro heritage was worthy of respect, and that this heritage was not relegated to the past, that its values were values that could still make an important contribution to the world.

R.D.: That is to say, universalizing values . . .

A.C.: Universalizing, living values that had not been exhausted. The field was not dried up: it could still bear fruit if we made the effort to irrigate it with our sweat and plant new seeds. So this was the situation: there were things to tell the world. We were not dazzled by European civilization. We bore the imprint of European civilization but we thought that Africa could make a contribution to Europe. It was also an affirmation of our solidarity. That's the way it was: I have always recognized that what was happening to my brothers in Algeria and the United States had its repercussions in me. I understood that I could not be indifferent to what was happening in Haiti or Africa. Then, in a way, we slowly came to the idea of a sort of black civilization spread throughout the world. And I have come to the realization that there was a "Negro situation" that existed in different geographical areas, that Africa was also my country. There was the African continent, the Antilles, Haiti; there were Martinicans and Brazilian Negroes, etc. That's what Negritude meant to me.

R.D.:   There has also been a movement that predated Negritude itself—
I'm speaking of the Negritude movement between the two world
wars—a movement you could call pre-Negritude, manifested by
the interest in African art that could be seen among European
painters. Do you see a relationship between the interest of European artists and the coming to consciousness of Negroes?

A.C.:   Certainly. This movement is another factor in the development
of our consciousness. Negroes were made fashionable in France
by Picasso, Vlaminck, Braque, etc.

R.D.:   During the same period, art lovers and art historians—for example Paul Guillaume in France and Carl Einstein in Germany—
were quite impressed by the quality of African sculpture. African
art ceased to be an exotic curiosity, and Guillaume himself came
to appreciate it as the "life-giving sperm of the twentieth century
of the spirit."

A.C.:   I also remember the *Negro Anthology* of Blaise Cendrars.

R.D.:   It was a book devoted to the oral literature of African Negroes.
I can also remember the third issue of the art journal *Action*,
which had a number of articles by the artistic vanguard of that
time on African masks, sculptures, and other art objects. And we
shouldn't forget Guillaume Apollinaire, whose poetry is full of
evocations of Africa. To sum up, do you think that the concept
of Negritude was formed on the basis of shared ideological and
political beliefs on the part of its proponents? Your comrades in
Negritude, the first militants of Negritude, have followed a different path from you. There is, for example, Senghor, a brilliant
intellect and a fiery poet, but full of contradictions on the subject
of Negritude.

A.C.:   Our affinities were above all a matter of feeling. You either felt black or did not feel black. But there was also the political aspect. Negritude was, after all, part of the left. I never thought for a moment that our emancipation could come from the right—that's impossible. We both felt, Senghor and I, that our liberation placed us on the left, but both of us refused to see the black question as simply a social question. There are people, even today, who thought and still think that it is all simply a matter of the left taking power in France, that with a change in the economic conditions the black question will disappear. I have never agreed with that at all. I think that the economic question is important, but it is not the only thing.

R.D.:   Certainly, because the relationships between consciousness and reality are extremely complex. That's why it is equally necessary to decolonize our minds, our inner life, at the same time that we decolonize society.

A.C.:   Exactly, and I remember very well having said to the Martinican Communists in those days, that black people, as you have pointed out, were doubly proletarianized and alienated: in the first place as workers, but also as blacks, because after all we are dealing with the only race which is denied even the notion of humanity.

A POETICS OF ANTICOLONIALISM

by Robin D.G. Kelley

AUTHOR'S NOTE: *Mad props to Christopher Phelps for inviting me to write this essay; to Franklin Rosemont for passing along key documents, commenting on and correcting an earlier draft, and for his untiring support; to Cedric Robinson for forcing me to come to terms with Césaire's critique of Marxism in the first place; to Judith MacFarlane for her wonderful and exact translations; to Elleza and Diedra for cultivating the Marvelous. This essay is dedicated to Ted Joans and Laura Corsiglia with love and gratitude for our "Discourse on Theloniolism."*

1. The first edition was published in 1950 by Editions Réclame. A revised and expanded edition, published by Présence Africaine in 1955, was later translated and published by Monthly Review Press in 1972.
2. Frantz Fanon, *The Wretched of the Earth*, translated by Constance Farrington (New York: Grove Press, 1967), p. 102.
3. Robert Young, *White Mythologies: Writing History and the West* (London: Routledge, 1990), p. 119. A compelling defense of Césaire's *Discourse*, which has influenced my thinking on this text's relation to postcolonial studies, is Bart Moore-Gilbert, *Postcolonial Theory: Contexts, Practices, Politics*

(London: Verso, 1997). He argues that *Discourse* not only anticipated Fanon, but works by Homi Bhabha, Edward Said, Wilson Harris, Chinua Achebe, and Chinweizu.

4. See, for example, A. James Arnold, *Modernism and Negritude: The Poetry and Poetics of Aimé Césaire* (Cambridge: Harvard University Press, 1981); M.A.M. Ngal, *Aimé Césaire: Un Homme à la recherche d'une patrie* (Dakar: Nouvelles Editions Africaines, 1983); Lilyan Kesteloot and B. Kotchy, *Aimé Césaire, L'Homme et l'oeuvre* (Paris: Présence Africaine, 1973); Jane L. Pallister, *Aimé Césaire* (New York: Twayne Publishers, 1991); Susan Frutkin, *Aimé Césaire: Black Between Worlds* (Miami: Center for Advanced International Studies, 1973).

5. Arnold, *Modernism and Negritude*, pp. 1-8, quote from page 8.

6. Quote from "An Interview with Aimé Césaire" appended at the end of *Discourse* p. 85; Arnold, *Modernism and Negritude*, pp. 8-9; on black diasporic intellectuals in Paris, see Tyler Stovall, *Paris Noir: African-Americans in the City of Light* (Boston and New York: Houghton Mifflin, 1996); Brent Edwards, "Black Globality: The International Shape of Black Intellectual Culture," (Ph.D. dissertation, Columbia University, 1997).

7. Maryse Condé, "Cahier d'un retour au pays natal": Césaire, *Analyse critique* (Paris: Hatier, 1978); Norman Shapiro, ed., *Negritude: Black Poetry from Africa and the Caribbean* (New York: October House, 1970), p. 224; Pallister, *Aimé Césaire*, pp. xiii-xiv.

8. Arnold, *Modernism and Negritude*, pp. 12-13.

9. "Lettre du Lieutenant de vaisseau Bayle, chef du service d'information, au directeur de la revue *Tropiques*, Fort-de-France, May 10, 1943" and "Réponse de *Tropiques* à M. le Lieutenant de vaisseau Bayle, Fort-de-France, May 12, 1943," (signed Aimé Césaire, Suzanne Césaire, Georges Gratiant, Aristide Maugée, René Ménil, Lucie Thesée), *Tropiques*, vol. 1, ed. by Aimé Césaire [facsimile reproduction] (Paris: Editions Jean-Michel Place, 1978), Documents-Annexes, pp. xxxvi-xxxviii.

10. See Michael Richardson, ed., *Refusal of the Shadow: Surrealism and the Caribbean*, trans. by Michael Richardson and Krzysztof Fijalkowski (London: Verso, 1996), pp. 7-15, 69-182; Franklin Rosemont, ed., *Andre Breton—What is Surrealism?: Selected Writings* (New York: Pathfinder, 1978), pp. 83-92; Arnold, *Modernism and Negritude*, pp. 12-13.

11. Quote from Penelope Rosemont, ed., *Surrealist Women: An International Anthology* (Austin: University of Texas Press, 1998), p. 137; Franklin Rosemont, "Suzanne Césaire: In the Light of Surrealism," (unpublished paper in author's possession).

12. Penelope Rosemont, ed., *Surrealist Women*, pp. 136-37. "Surrealism and Us: 1943" is also reprinted in Michael Richardson, ed., *Refusal of the Shadow*, pp. 123-26, but I prefer Rosemont's translation.

13. Brent Hayes Edwards offers an illuminating description of Césaire's poetic challenge to surrealism. While he sees Césaire's work as a departure from Surrealism, I like to think of it as a transformation. Brent Hayes Edwards, "Ethnics of Surrealism," *Transition* 78 (1999), pp. 132-34.

14. Jacqueline Leiner, "Entretien avec A.C.," in *Tropiques*, vol. 1, ed. by Aimé Césaire [facsimile reproduction] (Paris: Editions Jean-Michel Place, 1978).

15. Pallister, *Aimé Césaire*, pp. 29-33.

16. Reprinted as "Poetry and Knowledge" in Michael Richardson, ed., *Refusal of the Shadow*, pp. 134-145.

17. Rosemont, ed., *Andre Breton—What is Surrealism?*, pp. 36-37; Maurice Nadeau, *The History of Surrealism*, trans. by Richard Howard (Cambridge: Belknap Press of Harvard University Press, 1989, orig. 1944), p. 117; "Murderous Humanitarianism," reprinted in *Race Traitor—Special Issue—Surrealism: Revolution Against Whiteness* 9 (Summer 1998), pp. 67-69. The document first appeared in Nancy Cunard, ed., *Negro: An Anthology* (New York, 1996 reprint, orig. 1934).

18. Cedric J. Robinson, "Fascism and the Response of Black Radical Theorists" (unpublished paper in author's possession); Cedric J. Robinson, "Fascism and the Intersection of Capitalism, Racialism, and Historical Consciousness," *Humanities in Society* 3, no. 6 (Autumn 1983), pp. 325-49; Cedric J. Robinson, "The African Diaspora and the Italo-Ethiopian Crisis," *Race and Class* 27, no. 2 (Autumn 1985), pp. 51-65; W.E.B. Du Bois, *The Autobiography of W.E.B. Du Bois*, ed. by Herbert Aptheker (New York: International Publishers, 1968), pp. 305-6; Ralph J. Bunche, "French and British Imperialism in West Africa," *Journal of Negro History* 21, no. 1 (January 1936), p. 31; W.E.B. Du Bois, *The World and Africa* (New York: International Publishers, 1947), p. 23.

19. Césaire, Senghor, and their colleagues in the Negritude movement had been fascinated with Leo Frobenius, the German irrationalist whose massive

ethnography, *Histoire de la civilisation africaine*, provided a powerful defense of African civilization. See Suzanne Césaire, "Leo Frobenius and the Problem of Civilization [1941]," in Michael Richardson, ed., *Refusal of the Shadow*, pp. 82-87; L.S. Senghor, "The Lessons of Leo Frobenius," in *Leo Frobenius: An Anthology*, ed. E. Haberland (Wiesbaden: Franz Steiner Verlag, 1973), p. vii; Jacqueline Leiner, "Entretien avec A.C."

20. Aimé Césaire, "Introduction to Victor Schoelcher," *Esclavage et colonisation* (Paris: Presses Universitaires de France, 1948), p. 7; also quoted in Frantz Fanon, *Black Skin, White Masks*, trans. by Charles Lam Markmann (New York: Grove Press, 1967), 130-31.

21. Fanon, *Black Skin, White Masks*, p. 130.

22. Cedric Robinson, *Black Marxism: The Making of the Black Radical Tradition* (Chapel Hill, NC: University of North Carolina Press, 2000).

23. Arnold, *Modernism and Negritude*, p. 14, pp. 169-70; Susan Frutkin, *Aimé Césaire: Black Between Worlds*, pp. 26-27.

24. Aimé Césaire, *Letter to Maurice Thorez* (Paris: Présence Africaine, 1957), p. 6, p. 7, pp. 14-15.

25. Manthia Diawara, *In Search of Africa* (Cambridge: Harvard University Press, 1998), pp. 6-7. Although the specific topic of Diawara's essay is Jean-Paul Sartre's "Black Orpheus," he is speaking generally here about a whole body of literature that includes works by Césaire and Fanon.

DISCOURSE ON COLONIALISM

by Aimé Césaire

1. This is a reference to the account of the taking of Thuan-An which appeared in *Le Figaro* in September 1883 and is quoted in N. Serban's book, *Loti, sa vie, son oeuvre.* "Then the great slaughter had begun. They had fired in double-salvos! and it was a pleasure to see these sprays of bullets, that were so easy to aim, come down on them twice a minute, surely and methodically, on command. . . . We saw some who were quite mad and stood up seized with a dizzy desire to run. . . . They zigzagged, running every which way in this race with death, holding their garments up around their waists in a comical way . . . and then we amused ourselves counting the dead, etc."

2. A railroad line connecting Brazzaville with the port of Pointe-Noire. (Trans.)

3. In classical mythology Silenus was a satyr, the son of Pan. He was the foster-father of Bacchus, the god of wine, and is described as a jolly old man, usually drunk. (Trans.)

4. Not a bad fellow at bottom, as later events proved, but on that day in an absolute frenzy.

5. Jules Romains is the pseudonym of Louis Farigoule, which he legally adopted in 1953. Salsette is a character in one of his books, *Salsette Discovers America* (1942, translated by Lewis Galantière). The passage quoted, however,

appears only in the expanded second edition of the book, published in France in 1950. (Trans.)

6. The responses of the celebrated Greek oracle at Dodona were revealed in the rustling of the leaves of a sacred oak tree. The cauldron, a famous treasure of the temple, consisted of a brass figure holding in its hand a whip made of chains, which, when agitated by the wind, struck a brass cauldron, producing extraordinarily prolonged vibrations. (Trans.)

7. From the opening pages of Descartes's *Discours de la méthode*, as translated by Arthur Wollaston in the Penguin edition (1960). (Trans.)

8. See Sheikh Anta Diop, *Nations nègres et culture,* published by Editions Présence Africaine (1955). Herodotus having declared that the Egyptians were originally only a colony of the Ethiopians, and Diodorus Siculus having repeated the same thing and aggravated his offense by portraying the Ethiopians in such a way that no mistake was possible *("Plerique omnes, "* to quote the Latin translation, *"niro sunt colore, facie sima, crispis capillis, "* Book III, Section 8), it was of the greatest importance to mount a counterattack. That being granted, and almost all the Western scholars having deliberately set out to tear Egypt away from Africa, even at the risk of no longer being able to explain it, there were several ways of accomplishing the task. Gustave Le Bon's method, blunt, brazen assertion: "The Egyptians are Hamites, that is to say, whites like the Lydians, the Getulians, the Moors, the Numidians, the Berbers"; Maspero's method, which consists of making a connection, contrary to all probability, between the Egyptian language and the Semitic languages, more especially the Hebrew-Aramaic type, from which follows the conclusion that originally the Egyptians must have been Semites; Weigall's method, geographical this time, according to which Egyptian civilization could only have been born in Lower Egypt, and that from there it passed into Upper Egypt, traveling up the river . . . seeing that it could not travel down (*sic*). The reader will have understood that the secret reason why this was impossible is that Lower Egypt is near the Mediterranean, hence near the white populations, while Upper Egypt is near the country of the Negroes. In this connection, it is interesting to oppose to Weigall's thesis the views of Scheinfurth (*Au coeur de l'Afrique,* vol. 1) on the origin of the flora and fauna of Egypt, which he places "hundreds of miles upriver."

9. It is clear that I am not attacking the Bantu philosophy here, but the way in which certain people try to use it for political ends.

10. The name given by the French to the people of Indochina (cf. U.S. "gook"). (Trans.)

11. Isidore Ducasse—the title Comte de Lautréamont is a pen name—was a precursor of surrealism who, unknown during his brief lifetime (1846-1870) had great influence on a later generation of poets. He is remembered for a single extraordinary work, the *Chants de Maldoror*, a kind of epic poem in prose whose satanic hero is in violent rebellion against God and society. The disconnected episodes through which Maldoror passes are a series of fantastic visions, occasionally mystic and lyrical, more often grotesque, macabre, and erotic, filled with sadism and vampirism. The work as a whole has the intensity of a nightmare and seems almost to spring directly from the author's subconscious. (Trans.)

12. Vautrin, who appears in *Le Père Goriot* (1834) and other novels, is the arch-villain of Balzac's *Comédie humaine*. A master criminal living under the guise of a former tradesman, he is corrupt, unscrupulous, and single-minded in his pursuit of fortune. With cynical insight into capitalist society, Vautrin sees himself as no more immoral than the respectable bourgeois of his time. (Trans.)

13. From "Le Vin des chiffonniers" in *Les Fleurs du mal*, as translated by C. F. MacIntyre. (Trans.)

14. See Roger Caillois, "Illusions à rebours," *Nouvelle Revue Française*, December and January 1955.

15. It is significant that at the very time when M. Caillois was launching his crusade, a Belgian colonialist review inspired by the government (*Europe-Afrique*, no. 6, January 1955), was making an absolutely identical attack on ethnography: "Formerly, the colonizer's fundamental conception of his relationship to the colonized man was that of a civilized man to a savage. Thus colonization rested on a hierarchy, crude no doubt, but firm and clear." It is this hierarchical relationship that the author of the article, a certain M. Piron, accuses ethnography of destroying. Like M. Caillois, he blames Michel Leiris and Claude Lévi-Strauss. He reproaches the former for having written, in his pamphlet *La Question raciale devant la science moderne:* "It is childish to try to set up a hierarchy of culture." The latter for having attacked "false evolutionism," because it "tries to suppress the diversity of cultures, by considering them as stages in a single development which, starting from the same point, should make them converge toward

the same goal. " Mircea Eliade comes in for special treatment for having dared to write the following: "The European no longer has natives before him, but interlocutors. It is well to know how to begin the dialogue; it is indispensable to recognize that there no longer exists a solution of continuity between the so-called primitive or backward world and the modern Western world." Lastly, it is for excessive egalitarianism, for once, that American thinkers are taken to task—Otto Klineberg, professor of psychology at Columbia University, having declared: "It is a fundamental error to consider the other cultures as inferior to our own simply because they are different." Decidedly, M. Caillois is in good company.

16. *Les Carnets de Lucien Lévy-Bruhl*, Presses Universitaires de France, 1949.